Border Women and the Community of Maclovio Rojas

T0308891

MICHELLE TÉLLEZ

Border Women and the Community of Maclovio Rojas

Autonomy in the Spaces of Neoliberal Neglect

THE UNIVERSITY OF
ARIZONA PRESS

TUCSON

The University of Arizona Press
www.uapress.arizona.edu

ISBN-13: 978-0-8165-4248-2 (hardcover)
ISBN-13: 978-0-8165-4247-5 (paperback)

Cover design by Leigh McDonald
Cover art from mural of Hortensia Hernández using photo taken by local newspaper after
her first arrest. Acrylic paint on two 4 x 8 planks of wood hung at the Aguascalientes–Centro
Comunitario in the community of Maclovio Rojas. Mural by Elizabeth Huato (2002); photo-
graph by Oscar Michel (2010).
Typeset by Leigh McDonald in Granjon LT 10.25/15 and Helvetica Neue (display)

Publication of this book is made possible in part by the proceeds of a permanent endowment
created with the assistance of a Challenge Grant from the National Endowment for the
Humanities, a federal agency.

Library of Congress Cataloging-in-Publication Data
Names: Téllez, Michelle, author.
Title: Border women and the community of Maclovio Rojas : autonomy in the spaces of
    neoliberal neglect / Michelle Téllez.
Description: Tucson : University of Arizona Press, 2021. | Includes bibliographical references
    and index.
Identifiers: LCCN 2021021357 | ISBN 9780816542482 (hardcover) | ISBN 9780816542475
    (paperback)
Subjects: LCSH: Women—Mexico—Tijuana (Baja California)—Social conditions. | Women
    political activists—Mexico—Tijuana (Baja California) | Women—Violence against—
    Mexico—Tijuana (Baja California)
Classification: LCC HQ1465.T54 T45 2021 | DDC 305.420972/23—dc23
LC record available at https://lccn.loc.gov/2021021357

Printed in the United States of America
♾ This paper meets the requirements of ANSI/NISO Z39.48-1992 (Permanence of Paper).

I dedicate this book to my daughter, Milagro. You are true to your name, a shining being of hope, puro amor, and so much joy. Thank you for the lessons that have come with being your mother. I love you mucho.

Contents

Acknowledgments   *ix*

Prologue   3
Introduction. Structural Violence, Gender, and Autonomy
    on the U.S.-Mexico Border   13
1. Mapping Power: Colonialism, Gendered Citizenship,
    Land, and the State   27
2. La Frontera: A History of Subjugation and Insurgency   47
3. Social Transformation in the Present: Reinventing
    Community and Self   62
4. Maclovianas and the Shaping of Autonomy in the Spaces
    of Neoliberal Neglect   98
    Conclusion. *Cada uno su granito de arena*: Transnational
        Organizing, and the Future of Maclovio Rojas   131
    Epilogue   149

Selected Glossary   *153*
Notes   *155*
References   *165*
Index   *187*

Acknowledgments

THIS PROJECT HAS HAD MANY fits and starts, and I've incurred many debts along the way. I certainly would not be writing these acknowledgments if not for the support of so many people who have sustained me and my daughter since her birth. It is not lost on me that her age at the time of this publication—fifteen—is the number of years it took me to finally finish this book. Single motherhood and academic careers are not a perfect match, but I'm deeply grateful for this journey, because at every juncture it has allowed me to be clear about, and solidify, my commitment to this work.

For providing Milagro with love and care when I was away writing or researching: my sister Claudia Téllez a.k.a. *mi Yaya*; my nieces Maia and Marielle; my *comadre del alma* Breca Rodriguez Griswold Mariscal; my cuz Carol Askew; and the friends who are like family—Araceli Mejia, a. de la maza, Shaylin White, Mary Dudy, Melissa Schumacher, the Gordon family, the Langevin-Nadolski family, Mariana Palafox, and the several kind and loving babysitters who have been in our lives over the years—thank you!

For the intellectual exchanges, radical visions, and major encourage-
ment to complete this project over the years: Felipe Hinojosa, Cameron
Quevedo, Ceci Brennan, Xochi Flores, Aura Bogado, Cynthia Duarte,
Belinda Lum, Tara Yosso, John "Rio" Riofrio, Gilberto Rosas, Daniel
Enrique Perez, Marlon Bailey, Myrna Garcia, Bianet Castellanos, Julie
Dowling, Grace Chang, John Jota Leaños, Mary Stephens, Nacho Mur-
gui, May Relaño, Carlos Valle, Roberto Rodriguez, Axan Kuauhtli,
Nana Osei-Kofi, Sandra Alvarez, Frank Galarte, Satya Mohanty,
Tessa Hicks-Peterson, Maria Ayon, Dana Martinez, Jennie Luna, Ruth
Nicole Brown, Xuan Santos, Vickie Grise, Ellie Hutchinson, Molly
Talcott, Carlos Alamo, Natchee Barnd, Elisa Garcia, Jeff Juris (1971–
2020), Emir Estrada, Kaitlyn M. Murphy, Lillian Gorman, Ilana Dann-
Luna, Anita Huizar-Hernandez, Sohail Daulatzai, Anna Guevarra,
Daniel Perez, Patrisia Gonzales, Rachel Afi Quinn, Ada Wilkinson-
Lee, Lydia Otero, and *mi querida* Edna Viruell-Fuentes (1964–2020).

For reading parts or all of this manuscript at different points and
for providing incredible feedback: Maylei Blackwell, Jose Palafox,
Jonathan Inda, Moira O'Neil, Michael Stancliff, Maurice R. Magaña,
Manolo Callahan, Robert Soza, Alan Gomez, Roberto Hernandez,
Cynthia Bejarano, Sylvanna Falcon, and Devon Peña—this book
benefited so much from your insights. I cannot thank you all enough.

For the tremendous mentorship and possibilities that have been
generated by my knowing and being in community with: Lourdes
Arguelles, Cindy Forster, Gilda Ochoa, Chandra Tapalde Mohanty,
George Lipsitz, Alejandra Elenes, Bill Simmons, Emma Perez, Ale-
jandro Lugo, Danny Solorzano, Monica Casper, Gloria Cuadraz,
Paul Espinosa, Antonia Castañeda, Julia Curry Rodriguez, Danny
Solorzano, Maribel Alvarez and to Larry Emerson (1947–2017), I
wish you were still here to see this book.

To Oscar Michel, for allowing me to use his photography and for having the patience to see this project through fruition. *Se te quiere mucho!*

Thank you, Jordan Beltran Gonzales, for being a wonderful copy-
editor, indexer, and cheerleader for this project. I am grateful to the

University of Arizona Press for believing in this project since day one, and to Kristen Buckles for really being the one who saw it through with so much generosity of spirit.

This expansive Sonoran desert on O'odham land has taught me so much—my baby is of this place even if I resisted it for so many years. To those who share a vision of justice and have filled our lives in the desert with love and beautiful memories, I want to say thank you for creating family with me and Milagro over the years: Susy, Mau y Emma Luna, Melissa y Jose Delgado y *familia*, Anel, Natalia y Nico Green, Leah Duran, Isaac Saaedi, the Gonzalez-Schumacher family, Lyn, Francesca and Javier Durán, Liz Soltero, the Wertheimer-Cisneros family, the Stancliff-Kirsch family, Kim Mascaro, Brandon Yoo, Jenn True, Rosa Jimenez, Emir Estrada and family, Omayra Ortega, Juan Tarango, Esmi Sanchez, Carlos Santos, Alejandro Menchaca, Laura and Eric (and boys), Marianne Kim, Grisha and Eden, Raul Martinez, the Dudy-Bjork-Wardy family, Ballesteros family, Matt and Victoria (y Cielo), Alan Gomez, H.Q. and Crystal, Wendy Cheng, Araceli Mejia, the Thiesing family, the "Simpadez" family, the Kuauhtli family, familia Valenzuela, and Rudy Guevarra—gracias.

To the families of the Nahuacalli-Tonatierra, the workers, staff, volunteers, and other board members of the Arizona Worker Rights Center (2008–16), to all of the members of the UA-MOCOS writing group who were also always ready to throw a much-needed dance party, the Entre NosOtr@s Collective, Mothers of Color in Academia at the University of Arizona, all collaborators and artists of the Binational Arts Residency, and members of the Arizona Son Jarocho Collective—heartfelt thank-yous for sustaining me beyond the confines of academic life.

Over the years I've developed my ideas through the invitations to give talks about this work both nationally and internationally, and these experiences have all had a remarkable impact on me. Similarly, my involvement in the Future of Minority Studies, the Arizona Ethnic Studies Network, Mujeres Activas en Letras y Cambio Social, the

National Association for Chicana and Chicano Studies, and INCITE! Women of Color Against Violence, among others that I mention in the book, have radically shaped my scholarship and worldview. I am forever grateful for the interactions, struggles, and camaraderie I've built in all of these spaces.

I've taught hundreds of students at this point in my career and so many of them have had such an impact on my growth—shout out to my students at Arizona State University (ASU) West; Northern Arizona University (NAU); the University of Arizona (UAZ); the University of California, Santa Barbara (UCSB), research exchange program in Queretaro; the Vivir Mexico study abroad 2018 cohort, and the students who built community with me at the Guerrero Student Center here at the University of Arizona. It's been an honor to learn from you all. My brilliant graduate students and research assistants have all had a hand in this project, with special appreciation to Mike Cassidy, Marla Conrad, Victoria Navarro Benavides, Alejandra Ramirez, Diana Lopez, David Cid, Cynthia Nayelli Carvajal, Nic de la Fuente, Elizabeth Miller, Cristina Gallardo-Sanidad, Mariana del Hierro, and Brianna P. Herrera.

The Chicana Dissertation Fellowship in the Department of Chicano Studies at UCSB truly gave me an entry to academia like I hadn't had before. It was the first time I was able to focus on the craft of writing as well. I've received funding for research and writing to continue working on this project through completion from the New College of Interdisciplinary Arts and Sciences SRCA Faculty Grant at Arizona State University West (2006); University of Illinois Chancellor's Postdoctoral Fellowship Award in the Department of Latino/a Studies (2007–8); Future of Minority Studies Mellon Fellow Award (Cornell University, summer 2007); Division of Humanities, Arts, Cultural Studies Junior Faculty Research Leave at Arizona State University, West (fall 2009); Acequia Institute summer grant (2016); Frances McClelland Institute for Children, Youth, and Families' Latino Families Consortium Writing Retreat (2018); College of Social and Behavioral Sciences at the

University of Arizona Junior Research Leave (fall 2019); and University of Arizona Provost Author Support Fund (2021). I'm ever-grateful for the support and belief in this book.

Thank you to SAGE Publishing for giving me permission to use my article "Community of Struggle: Gender, Violence, and Resistance on the U.S.-Mexico Border," in *Gender & Society* 22 no. 5 (October 2008): 545–67 for parts of chapter 3.

The Division of Humanities, Arts, and Cultural Studies at ASU gave me a good start to my career, the Ethnic Studies Program at NAU brought me back to life, and the Department of Mexican American Studies here at UAZ has finally felt like home. Thank you to my colleagues—both faculty and staff—in all of these departments who have supported me in big and small ways.

The Chicana M(other)work Collective was co-created in 2014, and I want to thank Judi, Christine, Ceci, and Yvette for healing me and for collectively bringing into this world the balm that many of us need as Chicana mommas trying to survive a system that denies us so much. I am so proud of each of you and am deeply thankful for our bond, our offering, and for what we have found in each other through our commitment to our work and—most important—through our commitment to us. *Tlazocamatli. Las quiero.*

To my *comadres*—Maria, Norma, Zule, Tina, Alicia, Irene—I am forever grateful *del corazón* for our *comadre* nation, which has sustained my mindbodyspirit.

A l@s Maclovian@s—*gracias por dejarme acompañarles y gracias por dejarme compatir esta historia—especialmente a Hortensia Hernández por su liderazgo y sabiduría. Siempre llevo a Emma, Rosa, Lety, Hilda, Vicenteño, Jackie, Luis y a todos los demas que compartieron sus vidas, enojos, alegrías e historias conmigo—muy cerca de mi corazón.*

Jaime Cota at the Workers Rights Center in Tijuana (CITTAC), a long-time activist and supporter of Maclovio Rojas, provided me with important archival materials. Elizabeth Huato and Michael Schnorr (1945–2012) from the Border Arts Workshop/Taller de Arte

Fronterizo (BAW/TAF) were just as generous in providing me with historical information and important connections that would otherwise have made this task insurmountable; I'm so happy that some of the murals represented in the pictures of this book memorialize the important work they and others in BAW/TAF have done for and with the Maclovianas.

Estevan Azcona, thank you for your example in patience and for showing me what unconditional love and support truly looks like. You are a gift to me.

To my extended family both in Mexico and in the United States—*los Guerrero y los Téllez—gracias por el ejemplo.* To my *compadres,* thank you for helping me raise Milagro: Jaime, Yaya, Ricky, Kasey, Chava, and Breca.

I write this in memory of all of my ancestors, relatives, and wonderful comrades and friends who have transitioned from this world, but I would like to especially honor and acknowledge my parents, Freddie (1928–1994) and Cristina (Guerrero) Téllez (1936–2011), who truly taught me how to live my life with a critical lens as well as to value the everyday blessings of life—music, laughter, family, and the wonders of the world. There is not a day that goes by that I don't miss them.

Finally, to my absolute number-one rock, my daughter and *mi chilindrina*, Milagro Téllez. Mija, thank you for your support, your wisdom, your stubbornness, and for making me laugh like nobody else. Ever since you were a little girl, you commanded a presence that every single person that has crossed your path has noted. You've told me on more than one occasion that one of the things you'll remember most from your childhood is going to sleep listening to me either sweeping or typing. Thank you for your patience with me. You are one of the most amazing human beings that I know. I hope you get to live your life in peace, harmony, love, and with conviction. *Te quiero mucho.*

Border Women and the Community of Maclovio Rojas

Figure 1. West entrance to the community of Maclovio Rojas. Photo by Robert Wilde © January 17, 2000.

PROLOGUE

Somos un ejemplo de lo que está sucediendo a nivel nacional. En Tijuana
están privatizando la basura, los taxis, los yonques—así que o tienes que estar
listo para pelear o te rindes y la tristeza te consume. ¡Necesitamos encontrar
una manera de concienciar a la gente sin incitar a la violencia! Creo que si
nos organizamos inteligentemente podemos hacerlo, especialmente si somos
la mayoría, el gobierno responderá. Sin embargo, si seguimos inclinando la
cabeza, la gente como yo desaparecerá, lamentablemente no cambiaré, moriré
de esta manera. Somos como David y Goliat, somos David y la gran potencia
es Goliat, así que tenemos que trabajar para poder vencer a ese gigante. Es
difícil pero no imposible. Quizás estemos soñando, pero yo sueño mucho. Re-
cuerde, han intentado derribar a Maclovio Rojas pero no han podido.

(We are an example of what is happening nationally. In Tijuana they
are privatizing the trash, the taxis, the junkyards—so either you have
to be ready to fight or you give up and sadness will consume you. We
need to find a way to bring consciousness to the people without inciting
violence! I think if we organize intelligently we can do it—especially if
we are the majority—the government will respond. If we keep bowing
our heads, though, then people like me will disappear, unfortunately I
won't change I will die this way. We are like David and Goliath—we are
David and the big power is Goliath so we have to work to be able to beat
that giant. It's hard but not impossible. Maybe we're dreaming, but I do
dream a lot. Remember, they have tried to bring Maclovio Rojas down
but they haven't been able to.)

—HORTENSIA HERNÁNDEZ, RESIDENT AND LEADER OF MACLOVIO ROJAS, 2006

IT HAS BEEN TWENTY-FIVE YEARS since I first heard the word *autonomía*, or "autonomy." I lived in Spain in the mid-nineties, and the Lucha Autónoma of Madrid first introduced me to *okupas*, alternative social and cultural centers (*centros sociales*) in abandoned buildings taken over by youth in marginalized urban communities.[1] In an *asamblea* one night, an elder returning from a Zapatista community said to us, "No hay que luchar para destruir, hay que luchar para crear" (We mustn't struggle to destroy, we must struggle to create).[2] As one of my closest friends, confidants, and interlocutors Nacho Murgui Parra (former autonomist youth organizer of the Okupa movement in Madrid who, in 2015, became second deputy mayor of the capital of Spain as part of the Ahora Madrid campaign) says, "Es mucho más fácil destruir; se tarda mucho más en construir" (It's much easier to destroy; it takes much longer to build). All of this resonated with me for many years and became a philosophy that I have attempted to follow across my life as a scholar, mother, writer, teacher, and community member. It also raises a question: How do we creatively resist and build in community?

In the summer of 2002, I was trying to negotiate my time between my work as a doctoral student with my commitments as an activist across multiple projects. I had continued to be involved in support work for the Zapatista movement in Chiapas, Mexico. The year prior, Subcomandante Marcos of the Zapatista Army of National Liberation (EZLN) announced to the world that the Zapatistas were going to make a historic journey (*Zapatour*) to the capital of Mexico to meet with Congress in hopes of reaching a solidified agreement with the Mexican government after several years of negotiating about its noncompliance with the San Andress Accords. In some way or another, women, men, and children worldwide planned to take part in the Zapatour. In California, a caravan was formed that consisted of Zapatista supporters and activists from both sides of the U.S.-Mexico border; this caravan—for "Justice and Dignity"—was named Cosme Damian/Mumia Abu-Jamal, in honor of two binational leaders and activists.[3] I formed part of that caravan,[4] and, in March of that year, our caravan became a part of history when we arrived to the Zócalo[5] of Mexico City to welcome the Zapatour and its supporters. We were encouraged by the speeches, stories, and lessons shared with us and vowed to bring the Zapatista word home.[6] Those of us living in Los Angeles formed a Zapatista support committee and, upon our return, opened a small space in Echo Park to host cultural and social activities for the youth in that neighborhood.[7] We remained connected to a loose network of Zapatista-inspired organizations in the region—for instance, the Frente Zapatista de Liberación Nacional[8] in Tijuana, Baja California, Mexico—and, as part of our work of supporting and visiting autonomous community spaces, we organized a caravan to Maclovio Rojas, a land movement outside of the city of Tijuana that had declared itself autonomous. I knew immediately that landing there in that moment had radically shifted the course of my life.

Figure 2. Aguascalientes community center, during a celebration. 2003. Photo by author.

Llegando al Maclovio

When we arrived in Maclovio Rojas on that dusty summer day, my initial reaction was really one of amazement. As we approached the multicolored Aguascalientes—a community center and the main gathering space, I was completely taken aback by the fact that there was an Aguascalientes standing in Baja California, just miles away from the U.S.-Mexico border.[9] Inside the community center, President Hortensia Hernández and community leader Rubén García provided us with a passionate historical overview before Rubén led us on a tour. I was deeply inspired by the Casa de la Mujer, a support center for women. That evening, I left certain that Maclovio Rojas was the place of an intellectual, political, and personal convergence within my larger community of origin, located along the San Diego/Tijuana border.

Figure 3. Mural in Maclovio Rojas: "The land belongs to whoever works it." Photo by Oscar Michel. 2009.

I stayed in touch with organizers throughout the next year and got permission to return to write about the community. When I moved back to the border region in the fall of 2003, I began my initial field research—mainly extensive participant observation—in the form of active involvement in the community's day-to-day activities, such as attending asambleas, actions, birthday parties, and other celebrations. I developed relationships with many residents. Often, I became the chauffeur-in-residence for those needing a ride. I took the organizers on *mandados* (errands), to the courthouse, to Tijuana at a time when the buses didn't go that far east, or just around the community. I experienced Maclovio Rojas in the unbearable dry heat and slid in its mud when rain transformed the landscape into a thick brown pool. During the day I jotted down thoughts and observations in a notebook and in the evenings transferred them to my computer. Sometimes I stayed the night, but, initially, I mostly traveled back and forth from Chula Vista to Tijuana—about a thirty-mile drive each way.[10]

I undertook archival research investigating local and national press coverage, court records, legal documents, community files, and other resources in order to complement the ethnographic material and supplement my observations with historical analysis of political trends, as well as to gauge local support. I conducted sustained and extensive one-to-one qualitative interviews with ten women residents, ranging from those who were actively involved in the struggles to others who were bystanders to and observers of events; some were long-time residents, while others had arrived more recently.[11] I remained in contact with some residents and subsequently returned in the summers of 2006, 2009, 2010, and 2016, when I led follow-up focus group discussions and interviewed some of the leaders further. The stories of the Maclovianas (women of Maclovio Rojas) and their activism shape this book.

The truth is that when one has engaged with a project for so many years, one often loses sight of the impetus for the work and even starts to doubt its relevance. My life had changed, as had those of the Maclovianas. Between my initial research and this publication, I moved from California to Arizona and formed a strong connection to the powerful Sonoran Desert on Tohono O'odham land. As my new state of residence was besieged with anti-immigrant legislation, I found myself immersed in urgent new projects (Téllez 2011, 2014, 2016) and became a single mother, which drove me to research and write about Chicana mothering as well (Téllez 2011, 2013, 2014; Caballero et al. 2019). In each return visit over the next ten years, the Maclovianas marked my daughter's growth the minute they saw her again after months—or years—of being away.

I began this prologue with an excerpt from one of Hortensia's interviews because her words, as well as the stories of all of the women of Maclovio Rojas that I spoke with, are what kept bringing me back to this project—their tenacity, their insights, and their ability to defy the State and transnational companies that have shaped the possibilities of their own futures.[12] I was reminded time and time again that their narratives—and dreams—have epistemological

Figure 4. My daughter and me during her first visit to Maclovio Rojas. 2006.

value. As Stone-Mediatore (2003) argues, "It is through enacting and theorizing experience, storytelling, and more, that marginal experiences can be recognized as knowledge" (6). This project contributes to the already existing scholarship that centers the voices and stories of women community leaders and activists (e.g., Bejarano 2002; Brooks 2007; Hernandez Castillo 2016; Heyck 2002; Iglesias-Prieto 1997; Kuppers 1994; Ortiz 2001; Randall 1995; Talcott 2014; Thayer 2010; Trinidad Galvan 2005 & 2008, Bejarano 2002, Ferree and Trip 2006). Through their storytelling we gain access to the intimate details and movements of the lives most affected by global economic policies.

Throughout this book, I build from the testimonios of ten Maclovianas[13]—Hortensia, Paula, Elizabeth, Dora, Sylvia, Alma, Luz, Teresa, Juana, and Maria—who grapple with their social and economic roles and their activist engagements as a way to understand how they negotiate and transform power relationships, in the way that Bickham Mendez (2005) defines as something "created from below and dispersed within and through oppositional movements" (63).[14] Their subjectivities both shape and result from the institutional collective action projects they undertook. I also try to understand the varying levels of political consciousness between the leadership and the residents while highlighting how their collective identity remains intact (Melucci 1989). Their bonding experience stems from their need for a home for their families, a goal that drew them all to Maclovio Rojas from various parts of Mexico. While the women come from different places, and each woman is shaped politically, culturally, and socially by the state or region from which she comes, the common ground of their struggles for *la vivienda* (a home or dwelling) marks a convergence of their political subjectivities that is a significant example of the possibilities of autonomy in what I call in this book the *spaces of neoliberal neglect*.

Women are at the center of my analysis because the majority of the leadership and ranks of Maclovio Rojas are women. I am not choosing to ignore the men of the community; rather, I am highlighting the role of Maclovianas as a result of my research and engagement there. As one of the organizers told me, "Somos puras mujeres porque a los hombres se les caen los pantalones" (We are only women because men's pants fall [i.e., men are not as courageous]). While my open-ended, unstructured interview questions centered on how the women had ended up in Maclovio Rojas, their experiences with the community, and the nature of their roles in the community, it became strikingly clear as I began to collect their narratives that the subject of personal violence could not be ignored. In fact, in the first week of my field research, I was asked by community members to intervene in a tremendously disconcerting incident: a husband was beating one of the movement's leading organizers. I felt powerless and was deeply affected by the situation, as I did not have the language to understand the contradictions of women leading a social movement while remaining subjugated in their home lives. To experience that kind of violence early on dramatically influenced my perceptions of the space. Immediately the notion of fear and repression at multiple levels became part of the lens through which I examined the community. I came to understand that this is the lens the women use to examine their own lives, and, as they critique it, they act to make changes. In the interviews and my exchanges with them, *las mujeres* (the women) discuss their roles in fighting for their homes, their land, and their community's projects, and the ways they have learned to carefully navigate and respond to the violence that they face both in their homes and at the hands of the State and transnational companies.

Mohanty (2003) situates social movements as crucial sites for the construction of knowledge, communities, and identities, proposing that any analysis of the effects of globalization must place at its center the experiences and struggles of women from the Global South: "It is precisely the potential epistemic privilege of these communities of women that opens up the space for demystifying capitalism and for envisioning transborder social and economic justice" (250). Mohanty's framework helps me trace a history of neglect and violence by the State, rooted in a colonial as well as neocolonial patriarchal system that condones the domination over women in the home, in the workplace, and in communities. My ethnographic work in Maclovio Rojas allows me to examine these theoretical perspectives. Over time, I came to recognize how this community generates political resistance and new forms of working-class organization; this process is associated with the emergence of new knowledge and gender subjectivities among the women who live, work, and organize in the *poblado*. In this book, I describe how the development of a woman-centered political subjectivity developed in a manner parallel to the community's own development. As Hardy-Fanta (1997) has argued, political participation is, in this way, inextricably linked with the development of the political self, the insurgent subjectivity that I have found among the Maclovianas.

Home, land, and community become synonymous, and these concepts gain real-world meaning through struggle and their collective resistance. Maclovio Rojas is autonomous because *la necesidad* (the need) drove them to create for themselves what the State would not. In so doing, the Maclovianas have aligned themselves with other autonomous projects globally, especially the Zapatista movement.

I always imagined that I would return to reside in the borderlands of Tijuana/San Diego; I envisioned implementing programs at the Casa de la Mujer as I continued to build cross-border networks and spaces of transnational solidarity.[15] When I finished my initial fieldwork in 2004, I received a dissertation fellowship that required me to be in residence at the University of California, Santa Barbara. Days before I was set to move, I received an early morning wake-up call from Hortensia. She was still in hiding at the time, and because she would go through burner phones frequently, I could not always get in contact with her. I had already said my goodbyes to the residents of Maclovio Rojas, and word had gotten back to her that after months of working and learning together, I would no longer be in the community day in and day out. When I picked up the phone, the first thing

she said was, "¿Es verdad que te vas?" (Is it true that you're leaving?).
I remember the sting of those words, because I did not want to leave.[16]
Certain I would be back by the following year, I promised I would
return. But I could not predict the future and didn't know that fifteen
years later I still would not be back permanently.

I hope this book both honors those dreams we shared and built
together in that moment, and that it also offers a story of radical hope
and possibility. While the world and the border has continued to shift
since my last visit in the summer of 2016, the community of Maclovio
Rojas shows us how the project of autonomy challenges "power over"
(Holloway 2019) and instead creates "power with," in community
and through social relations. Their story gives us insight into how we
might be able to create the world we want, now. Certainly this is a
grounding vision for us to hold on to during these times of immeasur-
able grief and uncertainty, as we navigate a global pandemic. However, this moment in history has also reminded us how connected we
truly are.

Structural Violence, Gender, and Autonomy on the U.S.-Mexico Border

*Si el gobierno no nos da lo que necesitamos, nos obliga a que nos organice-
mos. Así que creamos nuestras escuelas, el campo atlético, y lo hicimos todo
trabajando juntos. Por eso somos autónomos.*

(If the government doesn't give us what we need, then they obligate us
to organize ourselves. So we built our schools, we created a sports field,
and we did it all working together. This is why we are autonomous.)

—HORTENSIA HERNÁNDEZ

MY STUDY OF AUTONOMY ON the border began in Tijuana, Mexico,
when I met Hortensia Hernández, a community leader and one of
several women who have been vital forces in fighting for the welfare
and prosperity of their marginalized urban community. "Mi único
delito es trabajar por la gente" (My only crime is to work for the
people), she explained to me over a cup of bitter black coffee one
afternoon in the fall of 2003. We were meeting on the patio of an
unfamiliar home located in a new development in Tijuana. This was
one of our many clandestine meetings during her six-year exile from
the community that she helped to create and that she had led since
she was only twenty years old. In December 2002, local police raided
Maclovio Rojas under the auspices of responding to allegations of

"theft of water" leveled by the State Commission of Public Services of Tijuana (Comisión Estatal de Servicios Públicos de Tijuana, or CESPT). Due to her role as a community organizer, the heavily armed police targeted and surrounded Hortensia's home; she managed to evade arrest by going into hiding. Three outstanding warrants for her arrest were issued at the time of the police raid. As she described it, "Mi casa fue rodeada por la policia como si fuera el peor o mejor traficante de droga" (My house was surrounded by the police as if I was the worst or best drug trafficker).

Her words lay on me heavily as I reflect on who is criminalized and what activities are deemed criminal in neoliberal Mexico, a country shaped and reshaped by the forces of global capitalism and the state of economic exception (Agamben 2005) that supports and extends the processes of domination across and within marginalized rural and urban communities. This is a book not only about the structural violence associated with neoliberal regimes, but also the creative forms of resistance by women and the communities they create and mobilize to resist displacement, subordination, and domination. While neoliberalism results in what Shiva (1988) has long called the "poverty of deprivation," my study focuses on the alternative forms of livelihood and grassroots self-provisioning—autonomy *en los hechos* (autonomy in action, or the deeds), as Mora (2008) terms it—that women like Hortensia have created in the presence of a failed state that, for some, has forfeited respect for the social contract forged in the 1917 Mexican Constitution. Given the long history of the subjugation of people along the U.S.-Mexico border at the whims of U.S. economic demands and desires, this book examines how these conditions unleashed the creative energy and movement for autonomy. What social realities created openings for *mujeres fronterizas* (border women) to take matters of organization, development, and community governance into their own hands? What lessons can we derive from the narratives of mujeres fronterizas' struggles for autonomy as a way to further understand the search by social forces on both sides of the border actively seeking alternatives to neoliberal capitalism? In short, unmet needs have led to unparalleled agency.

The rise of contemporary social movements for autonomy in Mexico became more visible in 1994,[1] when the Zapatistas sparked an international and national conversation with their insurrection in the southernmost state of Mexico, Chiapas.[2] These movements have continued to develop across the country today.[3] Many of the *municipios* (autonomous municipalities) across Mexico are comprised of Indigenous communities with a long history of self-governance, but a growing number involve more newly established *poblados* (land settlements) and *ejidos* (communal lands) that were created by the diaspora peoples of the North American Free Trade Agreement: the millions of racialized poor families and persons in both rural and urban settings who were displaced by the economic policies of neoliberalism and forced into internal and transborder migrations to survive in the midst of a repressive state of economic exception. In addition, in the context of resisting the increased violence on the part of the military and drug cartels, many of these autonomous communities have organized their own communal police.[4]

The central goal of this book—and radical genealogy—is to highlight the evolving *woman-centered political subjectivity* that I witnessed in Maclovio Rojas. Anyone who has worked closely with Maclovianas/os says that women have always led the movement (Mancillas 2002; Téllez 2008).[5] Instead of seeing border women as always sexualized, voiceless, and marginalized, the example of Maclovianas redefines them as active agents reimagining the political roles and responsibilities of women. As Mahmood (2005) argues, agency can be understood only "from within the discourses and structures of subordination that create the conditions of its enactment" (15). In Maclovio Rojas, the neoliberal state's neglect of basic needs and the community's response to do for themselves collectively triggers the processes that lead to the emergence of a unique form of subjectivity.

Structural Violence and Neoliberalism in the Borderlands

Over the last fifty years, the U.S.-Mexico border region has experienced profound social, economic, and political shifts due to policies enacted by local and national governments, the implementation of international trade agreements, and shifts in population—in other words, the global forces of economic and social restructuring. However, neoliberalism, as Brown (2015), helps us understand, is a governing rationality through which everything is economized; human beings become market actors; every field of activity is seen as a market; and every entity (whether public or private; person, business, or state) is governed as a firm. Through an ethnography of Maclovio Rojas, this book reveals how the reorganization of the relationship between racialized capitalism, society, patriarchy, and the State affected the working communities of the greater borderlands.[6] I situate my analysis within an extensive literature on women from the Global South and their participation in social movements against neoliberalism (e.g., Bakker 2007; Bandy and Mendez 2006; Barton 2004; Cuninghame and Corona 1998; Edelman 2001; Marchand and Runyan 2011; Mora 2017; Paredes 2013; Stephen 2003; Zibechi 2012).[7] While these projects span a wide variety of countries, organizational forms, and struggles, they all appear to highlight what Lynn Stephen (2003) has observed: "Many of these movements . . . [are] chosen because of the type of activism they represented . . . [with] a commitment to basic survival for women and their children with a challenge to the subordination of women to men" (1–2).

Likewise, I have focused on Maclovio Rojas precisely because of the type of activism it represents: a women-led social movement for economic and political autonomy designed to address issues of health, education, housing, nutrition, and security. The residents of Maclovio Rojas—and particularly the women—are on the "frontline" (Rycenga and Waller 2000) of struggles as they combat the structural violence unleashed by the neoliberal turn in Mexico's social and political formation. Following Galtung (1969), I am using the concept of *structural violence* to refer to the economic, political, legal, religious, and cultural structures and institutions that prevent a given person or population from fulfilling their basic human needs and full potential as human beings (see also Farmer et al. 2006; Hernandez, 2018; Mares and Peña 2011; Segura and Zavella 2007). Structural violence is analyzed in this study as a clear consequence of the neoliberal turn in Mexico, and its deprivations are seen as reproduced by what Foucault (1980) terms "assemblages" of the power structures of capitalism, patriarchy, and racialization endemic to the U.S.-Mexico border region (Anzaldúa 1987).[8]

This history of structural violence is manifested along the border through the death of migrants and the rise of *colonias* (unregulated subdivisions) and substandard housing, which have resulted in realities that women find themselves needing to resist and overcome. While colonias are unincorporated communities located on the peripheries of larger urban centers throughout the border region, they are significant as sites where we can study the peculiar assemblages of inequities associated with the structural violence of globalization of so-called free trade, industrialization, urbanization, and migration (Nuñez and Klamminger 2010).

Morales and Bejarano (2009) make clear that "the success of neoliberalism depends on the exploitation of local place" and "marginal local places within nation-states are among the first to be stripped of their resources by transnational economic forces" (425), such that neoliberalism is essentially a project of localized globalization.[9] The northern Mexican border region is emblematic of this harsh reality. Neoliberal privatization policies deprive border communities of greatly needed resources, public services, and infrastructures. Women bear particularly heavy burdens when the communities in which they live lack basic necessities, since they are the ones most directly responsible for cooking, cleaning, and, in essence, the reproductive labor of communities and families. When the colonias they live in lack potable water and sewage systems, even these tasks pose major challenges. Systems of gendered power leave women economically marginal while at the same time making them domestically central: they are held responsible for the care and upkeep of children, but are deprived of the economic resources and domestic infrastructure required to do so effectively. The cross-border disparities evident in the San Diego/ Tijuana border region are grounded in a specific gendered historical relationship exacerbated by global economic processes, or what Elenes (2011) has called the postcolonial geopolitical conditions of the borderlands.

Dolhinow (2010) has argued that the primary goal of neoliberalism is to redesign capitalism on an international scale and open the way to the triumphant return of "free market enterprise." Echoing the work of Bourdieu (1998), she argues that the central political project of neoliberalism is "to destroy all collectives" (Dolhinow 2010, 13). In her work on colonias in New Mexico, Dolhinow documents the ways that "activists are taking charge and working as individuals with neoliberal solutions to lead their singular *colonias* out of resource deprivation" (22). In contrast, the case of the poblado of Maclovio Rojas illustrates that despite the pressures of neoliberal ideologies and corporatist maneuvers that further their displacement, residents have effectively responded *as a collective* rather than as individuals, by drawing from their own rich traditions of self-help, mutual aid, and cooperative labor. These deeply rooted forms of social and cultural capital have allowed them to survive through the activities of a rich civil society that is neither created nor controlled by NGOs. Maclovio Rojas recovers as it redefines and remakes social relations. In a neoliberal model, there are no social needs—just individual ones.

However, the case of Maclovio Rojas reveals the inconsistencies and contradictions of power and neoliberal domination. Residents' commitment to their community at the local level compels them to scale disruptions at multiple levels of power and to create their own forms of social organization, economic activity, and spaces of conviviality. Thus, I argue that the self-organization and autonomist practices of marginalized women should be distinguished from the ideology of self-care, personal responsibility, and privatization championed by the advocates of neoliberal capitalist modernity, which needs a community of individuals. As Bickham Mendez (2005) explains, power is not just simple domination by external forces structured in dominance, but also something created from below and "dispersed within and through oppositional movements" (59). Bickham Mendez's approach to transnationalism emphasizes "the ways in which people 'on the ground' in particular social settings react to, engage with, and even recreate and influence global processes" (60–61).

While individualized neoliberal responses can indeed exacerbate global economic transformations, the community of Maclovio Rojas has consistently resisted the demolition efforts by a federal government in collusion with corporations and local government over the course of its unconventional survival against the odds for its more than thirty years of existence. The State insists on destroying Maclovio Rojas because it represents an alternative—one that pushes against the logics of capital. My study reaffirms an argument made more than a decade ago by Peña (1997), who insisted that "marginality is at the center" of the process of social change and the advent of new forms and terrains of working-class struggles for autonomy. Indeed, we find autonomy precisely in the spaces of neoliberal neglect.

A critical dimension of the difference between *autonomía* and neoliberalism pivots around the concepts of the individual and the collective—the relationship between people, community, and *cargos* (mutual responsibility). Neoliberalism bases free market fundamentalism on hyperindividuality and justifies it by reference to the extremist behavioral economics of greed and selfishness—qua rational self-interest—as the highest virtues that must guide the ethical political actor. Autonomy rejects this reductionist ontology and instead embraces the ideal of the person as a "dividual" collaborator intertwined with the institutions of collective action that create not just a sense of community, but the material infrastructure and social institutions that make the good life possible.[10]

In describing neoliberal transnational processes in the form of new waves of forced migration, shifting labor markets, and the influx of foreign capital, I demonstrate how the state of exception (Agamben 2005) involves a minimalist commitment to the social sector—that is, the State's failure to provide social services and local infrastructure— combined with an expanding national security and surveillance state. It is this new combination of a minimalist welfare state/maximalist security state that is exacerbating the structural violence endemic to the border region.[11] I am interested in highlighting what this has meant for mujeres fronterizas.

Ethnography and Sites of Political Resistance

Ethnography helps to illuminate the concrete instances where globalization impacts the local—in this case, the historical and geographical context of the U.S.-Mexico border (Buroway et al. 2000; Speed, Hernández, and Stephen 2006). Although ethnographic inquiry has proved to be an essential tool for social scientists seeking "to not lose sight of the people caught up in sweeping changes and global economic trends," and ethnographic inquiry "moves beyond abstract concepts found in contemporary theory to focus on the everyday lives of real people caught up in complex macroprocesses" (Chávez 1992, 3), it has nonetheless served as a colonizing tool as well (Said 1978). Writing "ethnographies of the particular" can subvert the "othering" process because it moves away from generalization and pretenses of objectivity (Abu-Lughod 1991). As a Chicana feminist ethnographer (Téllez 2005), I strive to respect the visions of the community by writing an "ethnography of the particular" while simultaneously reflecting critically on my own role as observer/scholar. My understandings fall into the tensions that many other feminist scholars have previously named: feminist ethnographer as dual citizen (Behar 1993), native (Russel and Rodríguez 1998), colonizer/colonized (Villenas 1996a, 1996b), or halfie-ethnographer (Abu-Lughod 1991), as well as the insider/outsider dilemma that emerges for people of color doing research in their "own" communities (Baca Zinn 1979; Zavella 1993).

When I think about my layered identities and experiences that have allowed me to establish relationships and fit in relatively quickly in Maclovio Rojas, I acknowledge my personal experience as a borderlander/transfronteriza (Téllez 2013) and an activist/organizer, my involvement with projects of autonomy, my ability to converse in both English and Spanish, and my childhood, which included frequent and lengthy trips to my mother's hometown in Mexico (Tomatlán, Jalisco). In many respects, I saw my family reflected in the families of the community.[12] Yet, while Maclovio Rojas revealed a world very familiar to me, the community was also far removed from my experiences and realities as a researcher. This tension constantly forced me to consider issues of power and privilege and the contradictions therein (Roman and Apple 1990). Over time, I came to understand myself as a scholar-activist who is part of a longer genealogy of socially committed research (Mora 2017) that might be best understood by the concept of "militant ethnography" (Juris 2007).

However, here I am also situating the stark realities of the imposed border. Because I have dual citizenship and can cross the border with relative ease, I recognize my own privileges in being able to choose to do research in Tijuana and the "class and cultural locations and implications that it produces" (Behar 1993). For example, on my trips back to the United States from Maclovio Rojas, when I reached the border crossing, my brown face, the old car that I drove, and my "accentless" English would momentarily confuse the officers, who were unable to immediately categorize me and make sense of who and what I represent. This creates the opportunity for an epistemic rupture, so, while the women I interview—Dora, Juana, and Maria—may not be returning with me physically when I am finally waved through, their stories, their spirits, and their voices of resistance come through loud and clear. This is the transcendant power of the written word.

Maclovio Rojas provides a compelling example of the ways in which local communities are creating cultural and political spaces for and by themselves and also directs us toward a new understanding of how a local project led by women can be *sustained through a reconsideration of political tactics*. Women have always been involved in popular urban movements, but, with the increased migration of displaced persons that led to the establishment of Maclovio Rojas, women challenged historical patterns and organically emerged as the leaders.

Beyond Fronteras

In this book, I argue that the physical U.S.-Mexico border is not merely a site of passage, a crossing line, or political boundary. It is also a space of resistance, agency, and creative community building. Literature on transnationalism has done much to illuminate the spaces created through transnational migration (Smith and Guarnizo 1998) and the important and necessary coalitions that are built across borders (Bandy and Smith 2004; Brooks 2007), including transnational feminist networks (Moghadam 2001). Yet, as border scholars Lugo (2000) and Ortiz-Gonzalez (2004) argue, it is also important to consider the border as a place of residence for millions of people. The unique sociopolitical experience of the border region creates the conditions of possibility for the emergence of a woman-centered political subjectivity that incites action and establishes the border as a space where transformative politics can take place. Following Castañeda (2007), I contend that while for women the borderlands can be a site of violence and oppression, it is also one of struggle and liberation.

The mujeres fronterizas of Maclovio Rojas demonstrate a shared commitment to collective action through the establishment and defense of an autonomous community irrespective of pre-scribed normative gender roles. A distinctly woman-centered political subjectivity emerges through their direct engagement and contestation with the State in their struggle for autonomy. Although Maclovianas may not explicitly identify themselves as feminists or proclaim their groups as women-identified, they possess a sense of self that empowers them to act and transform multiple aspects of their lives including challenges to gender roles. In other words, they question systems of power at multiple scales and across intersecting axes. Maclovianas speak to the emergence of a political subjectivity that identifies the ability to act—that is, to recognize the power of their own agency in shaping their lives. Their activism constructs political forms of citizenship that lead them to assert rights tied to national citizenship, such as the right to land to which they are entitled as Mexican citizens. Yet Maclovianas also disrupt nationalist discourses of citizenship by critiquing the neoliberal nation state and its ties to capital and transna-tional companies, expressing what I call *community citizenship*. As Sas-sen (2005) argues, the urban space of the global city is especially salient for the repositioning of citizenship in practice, generating dynamics that signal possibilities for a social membership that is simultaneously localized and transnational. Women—particularly Native and Mexi-can women—have largely been erased from the history of the border-lands (Castañeda 1990; Gonzalez 1999) and are rarely acknowledged as "active agents of history" (Elenes 2011, 35). The women of Maclovio Rojas articulate new conceptions of autonomy and give voice to the largely ignored experiences of hope, change, and agency at this political divide known as *la frontera*.

Structure of the Book

While I have outlined the structural context that gave rise to the community of Maclovio Rojas in chapter 1, "Mapping Power:

Colonialism, Gendered Citizenship, Land, and the State," I further examine the gendered effects of economic and political trends in Mexico and highlight the ways in which cross-border disparities are grounded in a specific, gendered, colonial relationship exacerbated by globalization. The community of Maclovio Rojas has been created precisely at the intersection of the global economic processes outlined in this introduction, the debt crisis and neoliberal practices in Mexico, and the subsequent forced migration of Mexican workers from the interior of Mexico to the border region.

In chapter 2, "La Frontera: A History of Subjugation and Insurgency," I underscore how the economic climate of the border region, and the gendered structural violence it produces, helps me analyze the way border women and their communities have responded to transform these conditions. Women are left to do the bulk of negotiations for their families and their community. Although informed by previous urban popular movements, Maclovio Rojas is also markedly different in that their battle for land and dignity is guided by their articulation of autonomy.

In chapter 3, "Social Transformation in the Present: Reinventing Community and Self," I contextualize the case of Maclovio Rojas within the history of urban popular movements (UPMs) of Mexico, emphasizing the continued presence of women and their roles in reconstituting not only their lives but also their positions within the State. When the leaders remind the residents "Lo que tenemos lo tenemos por nosotros" (What we have, we have because of ourselves), they are reinforcing an ideology of collective resistance grounded in not only a shared history but a shared vision for a shared future. This leads to a personal sense of power, which can lead to action and, ultimately, change. Maclovianas' actions are directed simultaneously at the neoliberal state and at the unequal relationships women experience within their homes, both being sociopolitical structures that condone violence.

In chapter 4, "Maclovianas and the Shaping of Autonomy in the Spaces of Neoliberal Neglect," I argue that Maclovio Rojas is another example of the power of collective action against the will, logic, and policies of neoliberal ideology, which seeks not just to privatize life but to limit how to imagine and create a different world. These local mobilizations are redefining the political actors of the world and demonstrating how globalization from above is challenged by globalization from below and in between; oppositional impulses and communities of resistance are thus disrupting the collaboration between states and the main agents of capital formation. In self-determining the future of their poblado, Maclovianas/os are demanding their lands—and thus their settlement—to be formally recognized, but also moving forward in developing their community according to collective goals irrespective of the approval of the State.

Finally, in the conclusion, *"Cada uno su granito de arena*: Transnational Organizing and the Future of Maclovio Rojas,"[13] I demonstrate that through my analysis of the lived experiences of the mujeres fronterizas of Maclovio Rojas, how collective struggles on the border not only work to undo the dichotomous nature of women's public and private roles, but also make evident the border as a transformative space, a site where women are coming together to reimagine and redefine gendered, class-based, and racialized social structures. Furthermore, in what may be one of the ironies of globalization, the ebb and flow of transnational capital and its effects across borders have not gone unnoticed, opening up the possibilities for transnational collaboration. While cross-border interaction has always existed along the San Diego/Tijuana border, here I describe how the location of Maclovio Rojas near the border also facilitated collaboration of transnational actors who, in turn, brought significant visibility to Maclovio Rojas that grew their networks of support and helped sustain the community.

CHAPTER 1
Mapping Power

Colonialism, Gendered Citizenship, Land, and the State

THE CITY OF TIJUANA HAS been central to Mexico's long history of urban popular movements and land settlements, where neighborhoods such as Colonia Jardin, Colonia Libertad, Cartolandia, and Colonia Tierra y Libertad emerged out of contested battles over space, land, resources, and political power (Valenzuela-Arce 1991). By 2014, 140,000 families still lived in disputed lands across the state of Baja California (Zulaica 2015). The community of Maclovio Rojas, the most notable and long-standing, continues battling for its land titles after over thirty years of struggle. Founded in 1988 by families who were members of the Independent Central of Agricultural Workers and Peasants (CIOAC), the poblado was named for Maclovio Rojas Márquez, a Mixteco CIOAC leader from Oaxaca, who was killed by a fellow organizer in 1987 under orders from a grower frustrated with Márquez's organizing tactics.[1] At the time of his death, Maclovio Rojas Márquez was the secretary of CIOAC in San Quintín. This land movement and two others in Baja California were named in his honor (Mancillas 2002).[2] Located between the cities of Tijuana and Tecate across 500 acres of land, the community of Maclovio Rojas is

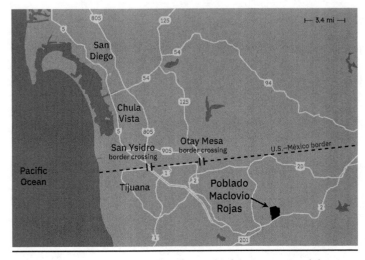

Map 1. Maclovio Rojas is only 5.5 miles south of the international demarcation. Map designed by Oscar Michel. 2020.

situated just 5.5 miles south of the U.S.-Mexico border. Twenty-five families seeking land and shelter founded the community on April 10, 1988, and since then the settlement has grown to more than 3,000 families.[3]

As I see it, Maclovianas/os' mere survival defies conventional neoliberal expectations. Although Maclovio Rojas is still labeled as an "irregular land settlement," which effectively denies legal recognition by the State and land titles to its residents, Maclovianas/os have created a self-governing board through a civil association they've entitled Unión de Posesionarios (Union of Possessors). The union consists of an executive committee (*el comité*) comprised of a president, vice president, secretary, and treasurer, as well as a support board, which includes directors of the various projects, such as the women's center, agronomy, and legal work—leadership positions that are central to the growth and sustainment of the community. This model invites widespread participation from across the poblado, where residents are central to decision-making processes.

Figure 5. Photo of Mural based on photo of the man Maclovio Rojas who was killed in 1987. Photo by Oscar Michel. 2010.

For the last twenty years, the community has unanimously elected Hortensia Hernández as the president, for her visionary leadership and their trust in her. While in the first ten years other organizers stood at the helm of the movement, Hortensia's continued presence is the embodiment of the gendered resistance that has been central to the community's growth, both in her work resisting the State and transnational companies as well as everyday experiences of patriarchy and structural violence. As one resident commented to me one afternoon, "Yo pongo a Hortensia a la altura de Don Miguel Hidalgo, Francisco Villa, etcétera, pues para ser dirigente de una colonia tan grande y bien organizada como esta, ¡debe tener las faldas bien fajadas!" (I put Hortensia at the level of Don Miguel Hidalgo, Francisco Villa, both prominent figures in the Mexican Revolution, etcetera, because to be a leader of such a big and organized community such as this one, you have to have your skirt on tight!) Through Hortensia's leadership and the materialization of the community projects, Maclovio Rojas has become emblematic of a woman-centered political subjectivity. In other words, by creating the

Figure 6. Community president Hortensia Hernández, inside the Aguascalientes. Photo by Oscar Michel. 2009.

community of Maclovio Rojas, residents have challenged prescriptive notions of nation and belonging where a woman's worth is assumed to lie in the children she bears for the nation rather than in her own leadership. Through women's active participation, a distinctly gendered political subjectivity has emerged.

However, to understand the case of Maclovio Rojas, one must first comprehend the long history of the northern border in Mexico in relation to the Mexican nation-state at large and global economic policies that are rooted in the legacies of colonialism. Here I trace these histories to show how autonomy—in the spaces of neoliberal neglect—is a remarkable response to the weight of history and the binds of structural violence.

Empire and Coloniality

Hardt and Negri (2000) argue that the constituted power of neoliberal states is marked by a permanent war economy that targets insurgent spaces and the poor multitude of the Global South for subordination, exploitation, and extirpation. This is the rule of empire and represents the late stage of global capitalist modernity. However, these critiques, worthy as they might be, downplay two specific dimensions of globalization highlighted in the case of Maclovio Rojas. First, the age of global empire does not spell the end of the "local" any more than the collapse of the Soviet state capitalist formation implied the "end of history" (Fukuyama 2006). Secondly, the particular positioning of Mexico in the global economy is to this day profoundly marked by its colonial history, which is the context of an inherited relationship vis-à-vis the United States, particularly during the Porfiriato, which I will come to shortly (Gonzalez and Fernandez 2002; Hart 2002). Cumes (2012) argues that the patriarchal system in Latin America cannot be explained without colonization, and colonization cannot be explained without patriarchal oppression. This has had lasting ramifications for the conditions and struggles of women, who may be seen as the "last colony" (Mies 1988) in a history of capitalistic empire understood as ongoing accumulation. If capitalism is entangled with patriarchy, women's resistance highlights its incompleteness.

In the contemporary global political-economy, states with a colonial history have maintained their peripheral status despite independence, temporary periods of stabilization, or economic growth. Indeed, the economic and political patterns of contemporary globalization ensure the persistence of this status. Diaz-Polanco (1997) and Stavenhagen (1999) assert that the colonial process, instead of developing a socioeconomic structure and an internal market that generated integration, created a national life where the exploitation and perpetuation of slavery and servility was imposed on Indigenous and African people throughout Latin America. The "illusion of progress" (Grosfoguel 2002) rested on the backs of this "labor" force, who were never considered a part of the respective national dialogues. In essence, the construction of national identities from the former colonies in Latin America ignored the economic and sociocultural plurality of each, and instead national projects emerged that were guided by and for the learned Euro-descended elite—not for all the people. Diaz Polanco argues that "ethnic or regional conflicts that might vaguely express sociocultural demands seemed an offense against the fundamental goal of maximizing the unity of the nation-state" (12). The implication was clear—the plurality of concerns from a diverse populace was subsumed to the interest of the white elite, often under the guise of national discourses of *mestizaje* that in practice placed a value on the move away from the African and Indigenous makeup of the majority.

Bonfil Batalla (1996) also argues that the false pretense of a unified "mestizo" nation created in Mexico its own underside, what he terms *Mexico profundo* (deep/profound Mexico). This Mexico profundo consists of the majority (i.e., Indigenous communities, mestizo communities, and large sections of the poor urban population) that have been dominated by an "imaginary Mexico" since the conquest. It is imaginary not because it does not exist, but because it denies the cultural reality lived daily by most Mexicans and instead is built upon its own aspiration to emulate other European nations. Nation-states base their legitimacy upon the idea that they represent a homogenous nation, in spite of the fact that often, once the state was created, it had to engage in nation-building processes aimed at the forced assimilation of its diverse citizens (Guibernau 1999).

Grosfoguel (2002), expanding on the work of Wallerstein (1991) and Quijano (1993, 1998), maintains that today the core zones of the capitalist world economy overlap with predominately white, European, and Euro-American societies such as Western Europe, Canada, and the United States, while peripheral zones overlap with previously colonized non-European people. The global racial and ethnic hierarchy of Europeans and non-Europeans was an integral part of the development of the capitalist world system's international division of labor. The dominant representations of the world today assume that "colonial situations" ceased to exist after the demise of "colonial administrations," which obscures the continuities between the colonial past and current global colonial and racial hierarchies.

Grosfoguel (2002) uses the term "coloniality of power," drawing from Quijano (1993, 1997), to explain the historical continuities of the racial and ethnic hierarchies in Latin America from the period of initial colonization to the present. Linking colonization to the contemporary global system is important because the persistence of a colonial culture in the present informs and constitutes social power today (Grosfoguel and Georas 2000). Coloniality of power is thus a concept that attempts to integrate, as part of a heterogeneous structural process, the multiple relations in which epistemological, cultural, political, and economic processes are entangled in capitalism as a historical system (Grosfoguel 2002).

In many ways, much of the relations of neglect and domination that are present in Mexico and, specifically, in Maclovio Rojas are informed by the continuation of this historical colonial matrix of power. Essentially, Maclovianas/os use a variant of "nationalist" discourse, in this case asserting the common bonds of *Mexicanidad* (Mexicanness), to insert themselves into the political process. By doing so, however, they subvert hegemonic definitions of national identity, because, as the racialized, working-class, and female poor, they were never truly meant to form part of that "nation-building" civic discourse—at least not in their current form as a present politicized subjectivity—in their own right.

Hortensia shared with me a story that underscores these contradictions:

En Octubre de 1995 había unos koreanos filmando nuestra comunidad y nos dijeron que estos terrenos iban a ser de ellos. Luego Bustamente, Fernández, Reynoso empezaron ir de casa a casa en la comunidad diciéndoles que había que evacuar porque Hyundai iba a entrar. Los representantes del gobierno llegaban a las reuniones para decirnos que

teníamos que ir porque estos terrenos ya no eran de nosotros, y también me ofrecían cosas, hacían todo para sacarnos.

(In October of 1995, there were some Koreans filming our community
and they told us that these lands were going to be theirs. Then Busta-
mante, Fernandez, Reynoso [local governmental officials] started
going from house to house in the community to tell them that they
needed to evacuate because Hyundai was going to be coming in. The
government representatives would come to the meetings and tell us
that we needed to leave because these lands were no longer ours, they
would make offers to me [to essentially bribe her into abandoning her
community] as well; they did everything to drive us out.)

What Hortensia reveals is the constant and continuing antago-
nisms between residents, the neoliberal state, and the transnational
companies that try to trick the women into leaving their lands,
through threats and impossible promises.[4] The interest of the neoliberal state is not el Mexico profundo, but a place in the international
market. The value of the land that the community sits on is more
important than the lives of the residents who live there. However,
while coloniality of power obscures and distorts alternative and
oppositional knowledge formations, it never completely erases them
(Tomlinson and Lipsitz 2019).

Economic Transformations in Mexico

In order to situate the matrix of land and power in Mexico, I will
outline a (very) brief history of the formation of the country postindependence.[5] Mexico declared independence from Spain in 1810,
though it would take eleven years before Spanish colonists would
concede defeat. Having overcome what was until then one of the
largest imperial powers, many felt they could take on the encroaching

U.S.-American settlers in the north. Continued infighting through the 1840s led to the young Mexican Republic losing half its territory in the Mexican-American War, ending in 1848. Only six decades later, its internal revolution would commence in 1910. The Mexican Revolution led to the establishment of the 1917 Constitution of Mexico, at the time one of the most progressive documents in the world, which included protections for workers, women, and children, massive land redistribution, in addition to numerous rights and protections previously denied to the majority of citizens.

The constitution established effective social provisions for the country and its citizens. Despite these protections and rights on paper, they were not implemented until the administration of President Lázaro Cárdenas (1934–40), a period during which access to land became fundamentally important. The land distribution during the six years of the Cárdenas presidency, some 20 million hectares—almost double what had been distributed in the previous 20 years—is remembered to this day as a watershed time in Mexican history (Camin and Meyer 1993; Esteva 1984). Between 1940 and 1970, Mexico experienced large, sustained economic growth as government policies focused on providing incentives and infrastructure for diversified industrialization and commercial agriculture. This time is known as "the Mexican Miracle," creating a new burgeoning middle class. Throughout this period, Mexico's cities grew at unprecedented and unexpected rates. Yet living conditions in growing urban areas deteriorated rapidly because the government was unable or unwilling to extend public services to outlying neighborhoods, many of which did not have legal land tenure. This intentional neglect coupled with a corrupt authoritarian corportarist system that managed and controlled Mexican society by sectors (e.g., working-class, Indigenous, urban) exacerbated the political and social divide that reinforced the institutionalization of structural violence that disproportionately impacted the lives of women and their families. Most of those disproportionately impacted were from the majority Indigenous and mestizo populations—the continued marginalization of the Mexico profundo.

Attempts at moderate trade liberalization began under the direction of President José López Portillo (1976–82), who used the petroleum reserve as a guarantee, diversified exports, replaced licenses with reduced tariffs, removed official prices for imports and exports, and promoted exports through fiscal incentives and trade credits to foreign countries (Pastor and Wise 1994). These efforts ultimately failed. The corporatist state had become dependent upon the earnings from crude oil exports and foreign investments, which had initially spurred Mexico's economic growth. By borrowing money and increasing expenditures—all predicated on future oil revenues—Mexico sustained an annual growth of 7.5 percent (Roberts 2001). However, the economic boom ended abruptly in 1982 when world oil prices plummeted. Mexico was faced with a severe balance of payment shortfall, an issue exacerbated by the overvalued peso. Portillo halted payments on Mexico's foreign debt and nationalized Mexican banks, blaming them for the crisis (Roberts 2001; Tornell 1995). Mexico was in default to international creditors, lending agencies, and governments, particularly in the United States.

Working-class communities were hit the hardest by the country's political and economic instability. The 1970s and 1980s were characterized by growing capital flight, escalating inflation, and the progressive devaluing of the national currency (Bennett 1992). When President Miguel de la Madrid (1982–88) took office in late 1982, he inherited a virtually bankrupt economy, a distrustful private sector, and a newly cautious international banking community. Between 1980 and 1988, open unemployment doubled, and between 1981 and 1987 the numbers of those experiencing extreme poverty rose from 13.7 million to 17.3 million (Chant 1994; Moyao 1991). Under de la Madrid's administration, the legal minimum wage dropped by an average of 12 percent annually, and together with the rising food costs and inflation, the real purchasing power of wages also dropped dramatically. Scholars highlight how working-class families survived the crisis with nearly nonexistent institutional support by exercising "self-exploitation": minimizing their consumption and expenses and requiring more family members to work in the formal and informal labor markets (Chant 1991; Cortes and Rubalcava 1994; Gonzalez de la Rocha 1988). In other words, this was a way for employers to exploit and gaslight workers while absolving themselves of any responsibility.

Adult women aged twenty to forty-nine, mostly married with children, increased their participation in the formal labor force from 31 to 37 percent, as well as the informal labor market, despite maintaining traditional roles (Chant 1991, 208). They often called upon their female relatives to help cover childcare and other domestic duties. Mothers also shouldered the expense-cutting efforts; they spent more time finding the cheapest foods, they made clothes, they put off home improvements and the use of formal medical services, and they cut down on their social activities, travel, and visits to family (Chant 1994). Women's survival strategies ameliorated the direct effect of the crisis, protecting families from both the State and global colonial powers.

In an effort to stimulate job creation and economic growth, de la Madrid undertook what Pastor and Wise (1994) refer to as the first phase of liberalization efforts in the 1980s: reducing the percentage of imports subject to license coverage, relaxing export controls, and adjusting tariffs. The import regime, which had been adopted to address the country's debt crisis and balance of payment shortfall, became less restrictive, allowing for freer trade with foreign nations. To the same end, de la Madrid signed the U.S.-Mexican bilateral trade agreement to facilitate liberalization and the elimination of export subsidies. Between 1985 and 1988, phase two of the liberalization efforts was introduced in the form of a new four-step tariff reduction schedule, bringing tariffs down to a range of 0 to 30 percent by 1988 (Pastor and Wise 1994). At the same time, de la Madrid began a process of selling off public industry and services, the privatization model that has come to dominate economic policy globally.

Liberalization and the Consequences of "Development" for Women

Political instability and social turbulence worsened with the contentious election of President Carlos Salinas de Gortari (1988–94) in a disputed election against Cuahtémoc Cárdenas.[6] Consequently, the sociopolitical exclusion and marginalization of the population was widely felt. To reestablish credibility after the Institutional Revolutionary Party's (PRI) electoral victory, Salinas reformed electoral competition and the PRI party by shifting to regionally based party organizations. In addition, building on his Harvard doctoral dissertation, Salinas expanded the PRI-corporatist system by creating a federal discretionary program called Programa Nacional de Solidaridad (PRONASOL) (Coady 2003; Laurell 1994), to promote "productive employment and create a security net for families." Whereas the PRI-corporativist system had traditionally organized in three sectors—the Confederation of Mexican Workers (CMT), National Peasant Confederation (CNC), and the National Confederation of Popular Organizations (CNOP)—PRONASOL expanded the reach of the state through newly developed government sponsored (created) constituency groups. The PRONASOL program essentially cut across constituencies, both expanding the corportarist state and challenging the power of the original three sectors. To note, though, there was overlap with the populations that received state support across the three existing sectors. The program provided services and matching grants that financed small and medium-sized projects to improve health, education, infrastructure, and productive projects (Niño-Zarzúa 2010; Stephen 2003). Badly underfunded, the program had minimal success due to inadequate processes to identify the most needy households, distribute resources, and evaluate itself. In fact, PRONASOL resources became a tool to maintain PRI support; resources were distributed only among autonomous social organizations that supported the dominant political party and refrained from independent political actions (Coady 2003; Levy 1994; Yaschine 1999). While the program effectively helped to shift the perception of the PRI as being the party that cared for its impoverished constituency (Laurell 1994), women disproportionately shouldered the burden of its ineffectiveness.

Despite social costs, Salinas continued to expand upon de la Madrid's liberalization efforts as he, among others, was eager to have "his" country be a part of the globalized economy. In Salinas's words: "Mexico would join the First World." Influenced by international funders, phase three of the liberalization efforts (1988–90) saw greater tariff controls, and the execution of a broader framework agreement with the United States in 1987 to promote exports (Pastor and Wise 1994). The austere economic restructuring resulted in public spending cuts, curbs on wage and employment expansion in the public sector, reduction of food subsidies, privatization of many state and parastatal enterprises, trade liberalization, and the increase of exports through production modernization (Chant 1994, 504).

The institutionalization of structural violence continued through Salinas's presidency. As a prerequisite to signing the North American Free Trade Agreement, he modified the Agrarian Reform Law (article 27) of the 1917 Constitution that effectively ended further *ejido* (communal land) entitlements when it was passed in 1991 (Nash 2001). Article 27 provided "peasants" with idle national land to live and farm on in the form of ejidos.[7] In fact, this was the law on which Cárdenas based his historic land distribution. While Salinas's reform did not force ejidos to part with existing holdings, it did mean that communal land would now be available for sale or rent to either Mexican or foreign companies. It failed to provide for joint titling and eliminated inheritance rights enjoyed by women under the original reform (Hamilton 2002). Additionally, it led to a process of individualization of land rights that has largely excluded women (Deere and Léon 2001, Talcott 2014) and encouraged sale of lands. Today the country's National Agrarian Registry (RAN) shows that 51 percent of Mexico's land is within an ejido, or collective agricultural plot, but only 1.3 million women own land within an ejido, compared to 3.6 million men—that's 26.3 percent of the total (Telesurtv.net, 2019).

The consequences of women's exclusion from land rights cannot be overstated, as property rights not only indicate ownership, but also represent a level of control, access to, and use of resources, and significantly shift relationships among people. Owning property or resources implies the capacity to call upon the collective to defend his or her claim to earnings or income generated by the asset (Bromley 1991; Meinzen-Dick et al. 1997). Women's access to this valuable asset allowed them to better generate, manage, control, and distribute familial resources in a productive way and could offset the government's inability to ensure the socioeconomic health of families through its programs and administration. Land rights comprise part of a larger process of empowerment, specifically the ability to challenge and "change existing power relationships that place them in subordinate economic, social and political positions" (Agarwal 1995). Exclusion from land ownership structurally stunts women's social, cultural, and economic development, forcing their dependence upon male partners and patriarchal institutions. Olivera (2010) finds that many of those women who do hold land titles are in fact widows who were holding the land until their eldest sons, heirs to the title, came of age. In summation, acute social issues of poverty, unemployment, the dismantling of the peasant economy, and migration accelerated under Salinas's watch (2010).

Because neoliberal reforms depended on women's reproductive roles being largely maintained in their traditional forms, "a large part of the *Salinista* project was the reduction in state expenditure thereby placing increased burdens on the family or, more specifically, women" (Craske 2005, 127). The neoliberal state demonstrated an interest in women's issues through gender legislation and through social welfare programs; these programs, however, only highlighted the political, social, and economic interests of the State rather than the real needs of women and families. Essentially, the State encouraged women to participate in the productive sphere while continuing to reinforce women's traditional roles as caregivers, thereby institutionalizing the extra burdens that conditioned the continued structural violence directed at and disproportionately experienced by women (2005). Here it is important to note that, in Maclovio Rojas, the creation of a woman-centered community-owned infrastructure can be seen in the completed projects. Moreover, women are prioritized when land plots are assigned, and instead of granting men titles of land, the titles are put under the names of the women, a practice that undermines the logic of the patriarchal state.[8]

NAFTA

Proposed in 1988 and signed in 1992, the North American Free Trade Agreement (NAFTA) further opened up Mexico's markets to global trade, which threatened and displaced small-plot cultivators who could not compete with U.S.-subsidized agroindustrial producers (Nash 2001). According to Sassen (1998), this shift is the single most important effect of foreign investment in export production: the uprooting of people from traditional modes of existence. The development of commercial agriculture displaces subsistence farmers, creating a supply of rural wage laborers and giving rise to mass migrations to Mexican cities and to the United States. Many migrants would arrive in border cities and those landing in Tijuana would, through serendipity and networking, find Maclovio Rojas. Out of necessity, migration and remittances have become a household survival strategy to mediate the low profitability of crop production following the liberalization of the economy through NAFTA.

By the time NAFTA was implemented in 1994, the economic crisis grew more complicated. Despite NAFTA's design, which made it easier for foreign companies to move money and goods across the border, U.S. investors were not satisfied with the state of Mexico's economy, particularly after the Zapatista uprising of January 1, 1994, that declared NAFTA the death knell for Indigenous peoples in Mexico. In their panic, investors began selling the Mexican government bonds that had financed the insipient step into the "first world" in 1994. When Ernesto Zedillo became president (1994–2000), he was forced to devalue the peso almost immediately after he took office in order to prevent a flood of money from going back to the north. From 3.1 pesos/dollar, the value of the peso fell immediately to 5.7 pesos/dollar. Interest rates on the foreign and internal debt climbed to 30 percent, as Zedillo agreed to a package of reforms mandated by the International Monetary Fund (IMF) as the price for a $20 billion bailout organized by U.S. president Bill Clinton. These reforms included more of what had been implemented during the 1980s: structural adjustment programs that further rolled back public spending and protections for workers; continued privatization of state services; and increased militarization of the country, not only in rural areas in response to uprisings like those of the Zapatistas, but continuing the tradition of militarizing urban police forces. All of this facilitated the expansion of the free market. Instead of producing growth and prosperity, Mexico lost 1 million jobs in 1995, the year after NAFTA went into effect (Bacon 2004), and, in the same year, the real GDP dropped by 7 percent (Niño-Zarazúa 2010).

Though NAFTA was touted in all three signator countries (United States, Mexico, and Canada) as a way to decrease internal and international migration, particularly from Mexico to the United States; to benefit small businesses and rural workers; and to generally bring Mexico into the first world, ten years after NAFTA's implementation, King (2006) highlights that 95 percent of foreign investment went to commercial farmers. Due to access to credit from banks, these commercial farmers could create the necessary infrastructure to change crop production to align with Mexico's export needs. Small- to medium-scale farmers were further disadvantaged, as they were least likely to receive income support through programs like PROCAMPO and Alianza Para el Campo, decreasing their ability to compete and survive after NAFTA (2006). King also points to the fact that economic expansion was limited to the manufacturing sector and particularly to the maquiladora (border factory) industry, yet, much of the job growth experienced in this sector has since disappeared, as manufacturing operations have increasingly been moved to Asia. Furthermore, despite job creation in the manufacturing industry, given demographic factors and the displacement of farmers, Mexico saw a net loss of jobs. According to a 2017 report assessing twenty-three years of NAFTA data by the nonpartisan think tank Center for Economic and Policy Research, Mexico ranked fifteenth out of twenty Latin American countries in growth of real GDP per person from 1994 to 2016. If Mexico had retained its pre-1980 growth rate, it would today be qualified as a high-income country; instead, 20.5 million more Mexicans were poor in 2014 than in 1994, a rate of 55.1 percent (Gálvez 2018).

During the crisis, to provide a safety net for families and ameliorate the effects of contractions in local economies after NAFTA, Zedillo's administration instituted a federal condition-based cash transfer program called PROGRESA (later known as Oportunidades) in 1997. PROGRESA aimed to reduce extreme poverty and invest in human capital by increasing school enrollment and providing nutritional supplements and health services to rural families (Coady 2003). By 1999, the program covered 40 percent (or 2.6 million families) of the rural population (Skoufias et al. 2001). However, an evaluation of the program found that it created greater demands of women's time to ensure that conditions of eligibility were met—that is, children enrolled in school and health clinic attendance (Coady 2003). The success of PROGRESA/Oportunidades and the improved welfare of families were in large part due to the roles and sacrifices of women. In developing countries across the world, the curtailment of social services marks an added burden to women who take on the responsibilities abdicated by the State, increasing the amount of unpaid reproductive labor they perform.[9]

State Neglect

Just as women are subjected to institutionalized and everyday external controls, so too is Mexico subjected to the control of multinational institutions and investors that intend to expand the globalized economy, as the influence of foreigners and foreign investment takes greater hold of the country. To illustrate this point, Harvey (2007) points out that "while only one of the Mexican banks privatized in 1990 was foreign owned, by 2000, twenty-four of thirty were in foreign hands" (103).

The economic structure of violence imposed on Mexico by the IMF, supplemented by the restrictive conditions required by U.S. bank loans and bailouts, has contributed to unliveable conditions for the urban and rural racialized poor. These loans are not available for social benefits; instead, they are made for infrastructure improvements in order to encourage investment—in other words, to reproduce conditions of capitalist value extraction. Those conditions require Mexico to reduce money available for rural credit, driving people into the cities, while opening up the market for imports of food (Bacon 2004). While Vicente Fox (2000–2006) was the first PAN (National Action Party) presidential candidate to be elected to the office of the presidency, and his historical election broke the powerful political grip of PRI, which had held onto power for seventy-one years, the dynamics of capital did not shift. President Vicente

Fox adopted a discourse that systematically denied the exasperating social realities experienced by the majority of the population, among them marginalization; social, legal and political exclusion in urban and rural areas; and a critical absence of human rights (Olivera 2010). The long history of State neglect contributes to what Ortiz-Gonzalez (2004) calls "persistent frontiers" at the border region as it becomes a site for continued colonizations. He states, "Newcomers and institutional bodies based elsewhere command greater influence than most local residents" (xii) and underscores the ways in which "the border region crystallizes the stunning ambiguities of globalization with blinding clarity" (xvii)—unequal reproduction reproduces inequality. In other words, while some argue that globalization has limited the nation-state's capacity to administer national economies (Miyoshi 1996; Safran 2000), I maintain that proliferating global markets have actually increased the need for national boundaries and monitoring. Borders have become more porous to the free flow of capital and goods but not to the free passage of people (Sadowski-Smith 2002).

Indeed, cross-border free trade does not apply to people attempting to cross the U.S.-Mexico border. In fact, the issue of opening the border to Mexican migrants was systematically excluded from NAFTA discussions (Adler-Hellman 1994). At the San Diego/Tijuana crossing point, this reality is most visible with the increased measures of security implemented with Operation Gatekeeper in 1994, the same year NAFTA went into effect, clearly demonstrating the ways in which the international demarcation has become increasingly more militarized (Andreas 2000; Dunn 1996; Nevins, 2002; Parenti 1999), effectively making it more difficult and, often, deadly for migrants to cross from the south to the north. This is most apparent in the Sonoran Corridor, where migrants attempting to cross the border have been funneled to the harsh deserts (Cunningham 2004; Rubio-Goldsmith et al. 2016). For women, it also means increased sexual aggression, attacks, and rapes (Falcón 2006; Simmons, Menjívar, and

Téllez 2015; Téllez, Simmons, and del Hierro 2018) in the migratory process. Segato (2014) argues that violence against women has "stopped being collateral damage of war and instead has transformed to a strategic objective of this new scenario of warfare" (15, translation mine) producing what Gonzalez (2021) has called the "femicide machine," or what Fregoso and Bejarano (2010) refer to as "feminicide"—a systemic process that creates the conditions under which extreme forms of gendered violence can occur without any kind of meaningful intervention from state institutions. As Castañeda (2007) argues, "Gender ideologies are pivotal in the geopolitics shaping imperial borderlands." In the following chapter, I examine the critical work of Maclovianas/os who are fostering a social movement at the intersections of neoliberalism and the weight of history and patriarchy.

CHAPTER 2

La Frontera

A History of Subjugation and Insurgency

MORALES AND BEJARANO'S (2009) POINT that the success of neo-liberalism depends on the exploitation of local place is best understood at the San Diego/Tijuana border, upon further examination of its history. Before the Mexican Revolution and during the presidency of Porfirio Diaz (1877–1880 and 1884–1911), the border region was open to U.S. investment and *latifundismo*, or massive land ownership. At the time, the Colorado Land and River Company and the Croswaithe, Machado, and Yorba families owned much of what is modern-day Tijuana after receiving extensive land grants from the Mexican government (Lara 2003). The Yorba family owned El Rancho El Florido, the land where Maclovio Rojas now sits, and where the Yorbas had previously raised cattle for export to California and planted thousands of acres for an olive grove (Mancillas 2002).

Given that the area on which Maclovio Rojas sits was officially declared national land by an edict of the federal Agrarian Reform Department in 1984—several years before the Salinas de Gortari's reconfiguration of Article 27—their solicitation for an ejido grant should have been a simple open-and-shut case (Diario Oficial 1984).

Figure 7. Looking northeast from Cerro de Esperanza in Maclovio Rojas. Photo by Oscar Michel. 2009.

However, their land struggle has been anything but. In 1991, the community paid the federal Agrarian Reform Department a deposit of approximately $1,000 in order to receive titles of communal ownership, but not until 1994 was their original solicitation denied on the grounds that there was no available land. The community leaders were shocked when, one year later, the neighboring ejido Francisco Villa was granted the 197 hectares of the Maclovio Rojas settlement, enlarging their current community (Mancillas 2002).

According to a national representative of CIOAC, "The Agrarian Reform Department violated its own rules by making this decision because the first entity to solicit a land title should be the first granted that title; new solicitations are to be honored before existing ejidos are enlarged."[1] This has created a conflict between the two communities, and the receipts of payment made to the department have proven to be useless in the case of Maclovio Rojas. Although their goal of establishing an ejido is still in litigation, the residents should have the support of state land tenure law: if idle lands are squatted on and used productively, then, after a period of five years, the squatters become the rightful owners of the land. If the land is under legal litigation—meaning that the lands have been held in bad faith, and other owners are making claim to them—then the lands are legally given to the squatters after ten years. After thirty years, Maclovio Rojas falls well into the second category. Yet, by making this a battle between two ejidos, the state continues to deflect any sort of responsibility, and residents of Maclovio Rojas must continue to fight for their land as their community expands and grows.

To support the growth of the community as they continue to make claims on their land, Maclovianas/os have developed several innovative tactics. For example, as a way of introducing new solicitors to the origin, development, and vision of Maclovio Rojas, prospective residents are invited to attend the Plática de los Solicitantes (Talk for new solicitors) that is given every Saturday. These gatherings not only provide leaders an opportunity to introduce potential residents to the community's history, but also to ensure that these new solicitors understand the commitments involved in living there. Members of the executive committee take turns running these meetings; they explained to me that they wanted to make it abundantly clear to any newcomer that Maclovio Rojas is a community "en lucha" (in struggle). I was present for several of these sessions, which often begin with a passionate welcome by a community leader:

> Esta es una comunidad en lucha, de apoyo. No vienes pagando, obtienes un terreno y lo que pagas es un precio simbólico, de verdad. Esto es para que puedas tener una propiedad familiar y mereces estar en un lugar grande, no apretado y endeudado. Trabajar se convierte en un círculo vicioso y mientras tanto el dinero va a los ricos. Aquí puede volverse autosuficiente, puede cultivar la tierra y existe la infraestructura para que se desarrolle como seres humanos. Nuestro objetivo inicial era aliviar la necesidad de que usted trabajara en las maquilas para que aquí se cubrieran todas sus necesidades básicas. Pero el gobierno

no nos permitirá desarrollarnos y, por lo tanto, cuando lleguen nuevos miembros, deben estar dispuestos a apoyar [el movimiento].

(This is a community in struggle, of support. You don't come in paying, you get a plot of land and what you pay is a symbolic price, really. This is so you can have family property and you deserve to be in a big place, not squeezed together and in debt. Working becomes a vicious cycle and meanwhile the money goes to the rich. Here you can become self-sufficient, you can till the land, and the infrastructure exists for you to develop as human beings. Our initial goal was to alleviate the need for you to work in the *maquilas* so that here all of your basic needs would be met. But the government won't let us develop and so as new members come in they have to be willing to support [the movement]).[2]

Right away, it is clear that Maclovio Rojas needed new residents who were going to support the struggle and be willing to defend their lands.

And defend they do. One afternoon, after sharing a meal with Paula, we arrived at the Aguascalientes and found out that Rosa Emilia from the neighboring ejido Francisco Villa had organized an action against Maclovio Rojas and rallied several supporters to invade a plot of land there. When others came out to defend the property, the confrontation intensified. Rosa Emilia verbally threatened Maria and her kids while a man in the group physically threatened Alma. I remember feeling a bit intimidated and fearful myself. But Maclovianos immediately went into action and organized an all-night vigil on the *terreno* (plot of land) that very night in order to defend and guard it. The *Villistas* did not return and that particular plot of land was no longer contested. However, their actions played into the hands of what was happening in the state of Baja California.

In 1989, Ernesto Ruffo-Appel, a neoconservative from the PAN party, became governor of the state of Baja California, in the first such win against the long-established PRI party nationwide

(Mancillas 2002). This impacted Maclovio Rojas in that the state's officials would not recognize any sort of paperwork exchanged with the federal government—including the payment that once had been made. As you will remember, because of the changes in the Agrarian Reform Law and in the mechanisms for the management of land tenure cases, the community of Maclovio Rojas never received its entitlements. Instead, its members were served with several criminal warrants and threatened with state civil procedures for squatting and illegal homesteading. Descendents of the Yorba family, as well as others who claimed legal land ownership, initiated these civil suits against the community and its leaders, a majority of whom were women (2002). The effects on the women were debilitating; many were forced to take time away from their homes and children in order to attend court hearings—or, worse, they were forced to take time off from their jobs, resulting in lost wages. In either case, the tactics were intended to wear down the efforts of the community members and leaders.

Additionally, Ruffo-Appel's first edict as governor was to endorse the No Invasiones (No invasions) campaign by criminalizing and discrediting leaders of irregular land settlements through new state legislation: "Crime of Instigating Forced Removal."[3] This made being a leader of irregular settlements illegal (Lara 2003), intimidating the leadership of Maclovio Rojas. In fact, through a targeted campaign in the early 2000s, many land settlements were dismantled.[4]

The tactics of displacement and removal by the state government aligned with the neoliberal market policies set up by the federal government with the intention of having land available to multinational companies. Bear in mind that, in anticipation of NAFTA, the Mexican Constitution was changed in 1991 to allow for the privatization of ejido land, giving private capital security and access to it. Barros Nock (2000) notes that, as a result, members of ejidos could decide whether to continue communal ownership or become private landowners; as such, they could use the land as collateral to obtain credit, and become associated with national and international capital. Multi-national companies took advantage and moved in. This is when the Hyundai Precision Company relocated one of their manufacturing plants to Tijuana's El Florido Industrial Park as part of a Korea-Mexico negotiation agreement that President Salinas de Górtari had signed to attract Asian investment to the border areas. In 1993, the Korean maquiladora appropriated one hundred hectares of Maclovio Rojas for storage and parking of their cargo containers and threatened to take over even more of the community's land. It is important, and not surprising, to note that the state government did not contest legal ownership once the land was out of the hands of the residents. To this day, the cargo containers remain.

Figure 8. Trailers that line the community. Photo by Oscar Michel. 2010.

Valuing capital over communities can be traced back to when the international boundary between Mexico and the United States was drawn, after the signing of the Treaty of Guadalupe Hidalgo in 1848. Tijuana was the largest of a series of small cattle-ranching villages distributed across the Tijuana River Valley in Alta California. The treaty bisected the valley of Tijuana, leaving to Mexico the hilly lands south of the Tijuana River's flood plain while the United States gained the flat lands near the present-day community of San Ysidro (Lorey 1999). Tijuana and Baja California were very isolated from the center of Mexico, where most of the country's resources, people, and political power were located.

The arrival of large amounts of capital into Southern California in the late 1800s had a spillover effect in Baja California, facilitated by Porfirio Díaz's government, which offered concessions to foreign capital to encourage investment—offers that U.S. interests took up, especially in the mining and transportation sectors (Nevins 2002). The most far-reaching transformation of the border region in the late nineteenth century resulted from the construction of a railroad network that connected the major commercial and population centers of the Mexican Northwest with the U.S. Southwest (Lorey 1999).

Although the border region abounded in valuable natural resources, control of its economy remained in the hands of bankers, investors, and corporations in New York, Chicago, Mexico City, and London. Essentially, as an economic colony, the border region sent its natural resources to more "developed" areas—always in the service of somewhere else, as Ortiz-Gonzalez (2004) also notes of the El Paso/Ciudad Juarez region. By the turn of the century, U.S. investments in Mexico had risen to more than $500 million. More than one thousand U.S. companies were engaged in Mexican operations, with more than 20 percent of their activities concentrated in the border states of Coahuila, Chihuahua, and Sonora. These investments marked the beginning of significant U.S. economic influence in Mexico (Lorey 1999). The transnational economic activity had a long-term effect on Baja California, engendering a heavy dependency on the United States and its goods, and vice versa. In fact, the original layout and orientation of the city of Tijuana was a manifestation of its intense ties with Southern California and the local tourist economy (Nevins 2002).

The rise of San Diego, especially as a seaport and naval base, fueled Tijuana's growth. In the early decades of the twentieth century, Tijuana's development was influenced heavily by its function as a source for the recreation of Southern Californians and the impact of U.S. capital. Furthermore, during the Great Depression, the United States deported hundreds of thousands of Mexicans, many of whom settled in Tijuana, which contributed to its population boom.[5] In 1942, the U.S. Bracero Program was established and attracted thousands of migrants to the northern boundary. Tijuana's population more than tripled during the decade, reaching almost seventy thousand by the year 1950. The post–Depression era coincided with a U.S. military buildup in San Diego during the 1940s and 1950s, providing a clientele for the entertainment and tourist economy that had been in decline since the Prohibition era and, later, the Depression (Nevins 2002). Clearly, the interconnected, yet asymmetrical, relationship between the border cities was defined early on, and Tijuana and its citizens were deemed second-class citizens, a designation that was reinscribed on the bodies of Mexican border women, who were seen as tools of diversion and exploitation.

Disposability at the Border: Maquilas and NAFTA

In 1961, when the Mexican government launched the Programa Nacional Fronterizo (PRONAF), or National Border Program, they aimed to beautify border towns, build up tourist infrastructure, and create "favorable" conditions for industrialization in the border region. The Border Industrialization Program (BIP), an outgrowth

of PRONAF, established the border zone corridor of export process-
ing industries (Herzog 1990; Lorey 1999; Nevins 2002). Maquiladoras were the only firms exempt from Mexican law, which required
majority-Mexican ownership (Lorey 1999). Essentially a pre-NAFTA
free-trade zone already existed along the U.S.-Mexico border; border residents had long been seen as the cheap labor for multinational
companies.

BIP also helped to fuel significant migration to border cities from
other parts of Mexico. In a forty-year period, between 1950 and 1990,
the population of Mexican border states multiplied 3.6 times (Lorey
1999). And the years between 1990 and 2004 saw an increase of some
24.1 million (29.7 percent) people in Mexico, 21.7 percent of whom
were absorbed by border states and 10.6 percent were absorbed by
border municipios (Institute for Policy and Economic Development
2006). In Tijuana, since 1980, the population has grown by 70.5 percent, reaching a total of 1,274,240 people in 2000 (Kopinak 2003), sur-
passing 1.4 million in 2010, currently at 2,140,398.[6]

According to a report published in 2003 by the Carnegie Endowment for International Peace, jobs in manufacturing increased
by 500,000 from 1994 to 2002, but in the same time period, in the
agricultural sector, where almost one-fifth of the Mexican population still work, 4.9 million Mexican family farmers were displaced.
This resulted in a net loss of 1.9 million jobs. If NAFTA had been
successful in restoring Mexico's pre-1980 growth rate, some scholars
argue that it is unlikely that immigration reform would have become
a major political issue in the United States, since relatively few Mexicans would seek to cross the border (Weisbrot et al. 2017). Consequently, after the implementation of NAFTA in 1994, predominantly
Indigenous Mexicans from the interior of Mexico migrated to border
states.[7] 64 percent of the migrants in Tijuana are from Veracruz, Chiapas, Sinaloa, Jalisco, Sonora, Michoacan, and Mexico City (Renteria
Pedraza and Spears Kirkland 2008). Attracted to the northern border
by an expectation of higher wages and employment opportunities,

many are dismayed by the unjust compensation they had received in the booming factories in the border industrial parks, as real wages are lower than they were when NAFTA took effect (Arroyo 2003; Audley et al. 2003; Davalos 2004). In fact, the national poverty rate was higher in 2014 than in 1994 (Weisbrot et al 2017).

Although there have been some recent shifts, historically women have comprised the larger part of the maquiladora work force through strategic recruitment efforts, due to a perception of women as undemanding, nonunion, and nonmilitant, as well as dextrous and naïve (De la O 2006; Dominguez 2002; Fernandez-Kelly 1983; Peña 1997; Sklair 1989; Tiano 1987). A 2004 study of 200 plants in Tijuana and Juarez offers a profile of maquiladora workers in the early 2000s: 50 percent of maquiladora employees were women with an average age of 26, their tenure was approximately 3.6 years, and, on average, they work at 3.1 maquiladoras in their lifetime (Carrillo and Gomis 2004; de la Garza Toledo 2010). A coalition of organizations that support maquiladora workers claim that the majority are "immigrants from Central Mexico and Central America with no experience in industrial jobs. Most are working women, many of them mothers or single mothers without extended families and support" (Maquiladoras 2010; Mendez 2012). Their seemingly endless labor in 12-hour shifts keeps Tijuana's 47 industrial parks, each employing 200,000 people, open 24 hours per day (Pool 2008).

Wage rates remain dangerously low, and overtime hours are often not paid. These conditions are exacerbated by the humiliation that workers face at the factories, where they are often required to agree to a set of rules related to dress code, bathroom use, breaks, and water consumption. Women's rights are frequently violated through random pregnancy tests (which can include their being compelled to reveal their underwear to prove they are having a menstruation cycle), and sexual harassment by their supervisors (Ortiz 2012; Téllez 2013). In fact, Ortiz (2012) has found that nine hundred women per year are fired for becoming pregnant.

The disposable and expendable worker becomes the norm in the profit-driven realm of the maquiladoras. Given the economic climate of the region, and the gendered structural violence it produces, the ways in which border women and their communities have responded to these conditions provides important insight into the unintended consequences of neoliberal economic policies.

Women and the Social Reproduction of Community

Essentially, the mere existence of the community of Maclovio Rojas has defied a history of systematic exclusion, and at multiple levels of neglect. While the effects of unfettered access to global markets has exacerbated asymmetrical power relations, the processes of accelerated globalizations have also produced local movements, or what Dirlik (1996) calls movements to save and reconstruct local societies, globally. The community of Maclovio Rojas has been created precisely at the intersection of the global economic processes, the debt crisis and neoliberal practices in Mexico, and the subsequent forced migration of Mexicans from the interior of Mexico.[8] Maclovio Rojas—informed by a history of previous urban popular movements, which I'll review in the next chapter—is also markedly different in that their battle for land and dignity (using Holloway's [2019] articulation of dignity as the refusal to accept humiliation, oppression, exploitation, and dehumanization) is guided by their articulation of autonomy. Furthermore, the residents are confronting not only the state government but also the transnational companies interested in usurping their land.

I spent a lot of time in the Casa de la Mujer, which offered child care in two shifts (morning and night) for many of the mothers of Maclovio Rojas who worked in the nearby maquiladoras. Depending on which factory they had to travel to (sometimes companies would arrange for pickups), they would often have to take two buses to get to work. They paid a nominal fee of ten dollars a week to leave their children for up to twelve hours at a time. This covered the food in bulk that Nadia, the then head of the center, bought to feed the children. It was an imperfect system, to be sure, but it supported mothers.

One evening, I was with Dora up in the Vías section for an *asamblea* (meeting) that she had organized with that section as a way to to keep all residents informed. There were about twenty people gathered in the dirt, some sitting, near the hanging light bulb on the corner of the street where Dora spoke, motivating them. She had a community member read an article from the previous day's newspaper about the way the government used supposed "cholos" to burn a community out of their properties. She told them that they had to be united because if this were to happen they had to defend their lands together. I noticed the reciprocal interactions in the community meetings: Dora asked residents their opinions, their thoughts on how they should handle particular situations, and they always responded with a call for unity. Individuals also shared their stories of struggle, their reasons for living in Maclovio. The meetings that I attended usually started out with an agreement on the agenda, previously set by the executive committee, but finalized and agreed upon together. The meetings, Dora told me, are to "concientizar" the people—to raise their consciousness and constantly remind them that the work they must do together is not over. She is an example of the women who have been at the forefront of the struggle, through their visibility in leadership positions, on the front lines of marches and highway takeovers, and by their unwavering commitment.

Speaking from La Frontera: Border Women on the Front Lines

Residents argue that *la lucha* (the struggle) of Maclovio Rojas has always belonged to the women—that they are the ones *en frente* (in front). Men are present but not as visible or active. As community leader Hortensia contended in an interview, "Creo que en Maclovio Rojas, 80 porciento de la lucha ha sido llevada por las mujeres" (I think that in Maclovio Rojas, 80 percent of the struggle has been moved forward by women). Their mere presence as leaders challenges traditional gender roles and expectations. Some believe that women are in front because they are *más entronas*, or more daring, while others feel that the women's realm is more closely connected to the home—therefore, their responsibility as women is to defend it. As Sylvia asserted passionately, "Si alguien me trata de quitar de aquí es obvio que voy a pelear con dientes y uñas porque si no dónde voy a llevar a mis hijos?!" (If someone tries to remove me from here,

Figure 9. "Mr. Governor, show your human face." Photo by Oscar Michel. 2010.

it's obvious that I will fight with teeth and nails because, otherwise, where am I going to take my children?!) But beyond the women being more daring, or simply seeing their activism as an extension of their responsibilities to the home, Maclovianas recognize the larger impact of their work. As Dora stated,

Es grande, tienes un gran compromiso con la gente. . . . Ser parte de este movimiento, requiere mucho tiempo, dedicación, carácter, fundación, diciplina, educación y si no tienes una educación; pues debes de tener práctica y nociones de cómo entender qué de grande es esto. No puedes dejar de mejorarte, ir adelante.

(It's big, you have a huge commitment to the people. . . . Being a part of this movement, requires a lot of time, dedication, character, foundation, discipline, education and if you don't have an education; then you must have practice and notions of how to understand how big this is. You can't stop trying to improve yourself, to move forward.)

As I reflect on their words, it occurs to me that the women of Maclovio Rojas are expressing elements of an emergent political subjectivity, forged from their own experiences of agency and struggle in the spaces of neoliberal neglect. This is a response to a peculiar type of condition: their community is both the object of systemic neglect and also intense surveillance and disciplining by the neoliberal state. The construction of Maclovio Rojas as a political and social commons poses entirely novel possibilities for the strategies and dynamics of survival and endurance, and the alternative forms of social life emerging in what is emerging as the contours of a postneoliberal world.[9] When Dora narrates her vision of the qualities required to "be part of this movement"—qualities like "dedication, character, foundation, discipline . . . [and] understanding how big this is"—she is conveying the elements of this newfound and emergent political subjectivity.

For example, one does not get a sense that Sylvia or the other women are primarily concerned with issues that the liberal mindset might label as "gender" issues. Yet these women are transforming gender as a direct lived experience and performance—not so much as part of a movement for "women's liberation" as a pathway to collective empowerment toward community autonomy. Through this experience, their subjectivities both have been shaped by and are a result of collective action. I am reminded of the Bolivian social movement of "community feminism," which is based on the participation of women and men in a community without a hierarchical relationship between them, with both having an equivalent level of political representation. As Paredes (2013) writes, "In these times where borders demonstrate their controlling function of separating and making enemies of the sister and brother in benefit of capital, we instead create spaces where silenced voices can talk about the resistance and energy inverted toward the vital goal of building the good life on the planet" (37). Maclovio Rojas presents itself as a similar example of women's leadership invested in the broader survival of the community as a whole. For Maclovianas, this is what the "the good life" means.

CHAPTER 3

Social Transformation in the Present

Reinventing Community and Self

Como mujeres tenemos mucha energía, como mujeres nada es imposible, y como mujeres lo vamos a hacer, no estoy bajando a los hombres porque son muy queridos y todas necesitamos alguien a nuestra lado, son tan importantes como las mujeres.

(As women we have a lot of energy, as women nothing is impossible and as women we are going to make it; and I'm not putting men down because they are very loved and we all need someone by our side; they are just as important as women.)

—HORTENSIA HERNÁNDEZ

NORTHERN MEXICO BORDER CITIES ARE uniquely situated: alienated from the center of the country, and bearing the wounds of a long colonial history that has informed the region, its population, and the relations between the two nation-states.[1] Baja California is the place where Ricardo and Enrique Flores Magon launched a socialist-anarchist revolution in January 1911. El Partido Liberal Mexicano (The Mexican Liberal Party) controlled the Mexican border between the Colorado River and the Pacific Ocean until June of that same year (Martinez 1988). Women placed their emancipation at the center of the anarchist cause through the use of print media (*El Obrero*, *La Voz de la Mujer*, *Pluma Roja*), adding a gender discourse to the revolutionary agenda (Lomas 2007).

Maclovio Rojas forms part of this history along the border, but it also draws from the long-standing presence of urban and worker movements throughout Mexico. In the 1930s, popular movements grew out of the dissatisfaction with the federal bureaucracy, its lack of responsiveness and efficiency—especially in service provision—and the lack of representation among the political elite (Drukier 1995). In the late 1950s and early 1960s, organizations such as the Partido Revolucionario Obrero Clandestino-Union del Pueblo (Revolutionary Workers Clandestine Union of the People, or PROCUP), Partido Obrero Clandestino Unión del Pueblo-Partido de los Pobres (Clandestine Workers Party Union of the People-Party of the Poor, or PROCUP-PDLP), and the Partido de los Pobres (Party of the Poor, or PP) emerged, reacting strongly to economic discontent.[2] In the 1970s, resistance was manifested by urban movements such as Proletarian Line, Politica Popular, and urban guerrilla formations like the Liga 23 de Septiembre, in addition to landless movements in Mexico City, Morelos, Oaxaca, Puebla, Veracruz, and other states in Mexico. Also, various collective projects organized to solve smaller problems and, on a number of issues, began linking the local concerns to the broader national picture. Multiple autonomous National Coordinating Bodies emerged, which became known as the *coordinadoras* (Watson 2002).

These movements focused on a number of issues that prefigured what would happen in Maclovio Rojas. For example, La Coordinadora Nacional de Trabajadores de la Educación (National Coordination of Education Workers, or CNTE) called for more local and national democracy. The Lázaro Cárdenas Ejido Unión (Land Union of Lazaro Cardenas, or ULEC) fought for the right to a major government fertilizer distributorship and prompted other peasant-managed projects such as food councils, community-managed housing, and crop price mobilizations. La Coordinadora Nacional Plan de Ayala (National Coordination Plan Ayala, or CNPA) forged civilian resistance groups, while the Coordinadora Nacional del Movimiento Urbano Popular (National Coordination of Urban Popular

Movements, or CONAMUP) was set up in 1980 with the expressed aim to coordinate radical actions and agendas in the larger city neighborhoods. The Unión Nacional de Organizaciones Regionales Campesinas Autónomas (National Union of Autonomous Regional Peasant Organizations, or UNORCA) aimed to open up new critical spaces in rural areas on issues of land and democracy, and, in 1979, La Frente Nacional por la Libertad y los Derechos de las Mujeres (The National Front Women's Rights and Liberty, or FNALIDM) was also formed. Proletarian Line helped organize campesinos during the late 1970s along with groups such as the People United, La Central Independiente de Obreros Agrícolas y Campesinos (The Independent Organization of Agricultural Workers and Peasants, or CIOAC), and the Peasant-Mexican Communist Party, or CIOAC-PWM (Watson 2002).

Bennett (1992) divides urban popular movements (UPMs) into three waves, the first taking shape in the early 1970s. She argues that rapid urbanization due to rural to urban migration exacerbated the crisis felt in the poor urban areas as land tenure and housing systems were inadequate to manage the population growth. Land settlement generally occurred in one of two ways: the illegal sale and subdivision of communal or ejido land, or land invasion—the taking over of federal or private land previously viewed as uninhabitable due to the terrain, making service provision difficult and expensive (Pezzoli 1987). To gain party support, regularization became a political tool to replace land reform. Without consistent access to drainage, garbage removal, sewage service, water, electricity, education, health care services, and public transportation, residents of new settlements began to increase their demands to a government that became less able and more unwilling to meet their needs and, at times, even responded to them with violence. Women began to organize collective action through their social networks to force government action and were often supported by militant students who strategically supported grassroots horizontal coalitions that faced land invasions and increasing water rates (Craig 1990). Stephen

(1992) notes that, in the 1970s, women were serving on the frontlines, at first without recognition or decision-making power. However, in the cases of CONAMUP, UELC, and CNPA, women formed their own councils or commissions within the organizations both to represent their interests and to create space for dialogue and action, though not without resistance and violence from their partners. When women organized semiautonomously and succeeded in integrating, they were able to raise questions about traditionally accepted notions of work and roles, and initiate change (Stephen 2003). From 1976 to 1978, the development of urban popular movements decreased, primarily in response to an increase in repression due to the fact that Mexico had entered a period of inflationary recession, the government's response being to cut the social welfare budget. This gave way to a policy of repressing movements, eradicating squatter settlements, and co-opting their leaders (Bennett 1992).

The second wave occurred from 1979 to 1983, when the formation of independent popular urban neighborhoods steadily increased throughout Mexico, especially in the creation of neighborhood-based organizations and in the structuring of regional and even national coalitions of urban popular movements, which provided formal mechanisms for negotiations with the State. Due to their greater involvement and presence in the community, as well as deeper social networks, women were more equipped and efficient at utilizing the new organizations to meet their needs. Yet, due to the temporary nature of their organization, their creativity, involvement, and leadership continued largely unrecognized (Bennett 1992; Drukier 1995; Logan 1990), as, once the issues were resolved, women "[faded] back into the daily life of the neighborhood" (Logan 1990, 154).

The third wave of UPMs started in 1985, in response to the September earthquake in Mexico City that left 350,000 people homeless. In the aftermath of the disaster, the government's inadequate response reinvigorated the UPMs, demanding the reconstruction of homes (Davis 1990). The newly born Coordinadora Única de Damnificados

(Only Committee of Victims, or CUD) connected victims and activists across class lines, making state repression against the organization impossible. Cleaver (1987), in his observation of community organization post-earthquake in one of the poorest neighborhoods of Mexico City, writes,

> What I discovered in Tepito was a vivid illustration of how people could participate in the capitalist market economy yet subordinate that participation to their own needs. How instead of being caught up in the logic of the market, of profit making, of ever more work, of a consumerist approach to life, they could limit their work of production and selling to whatever was required to permit their real life activities: personal interaction, collective self-organization, intense struggle against the Mexican state for the preservation of their autonomy and the continuous elaboration of their own ways of being and interrelating to each others and the to the rest of Mexico. Tepito fought and lived, not alone and isolated, but connected to other communities in struggle in both urban and rural Mexico through a complex network of personal and political ties.

By 1988, participants in these actions had two decades of experience of organizing autonomous or dissident movements. Formal organizations that were independent of the PRI—each with their respective leaders, bylaws, meetings, ideologies, goals, and strategies—existed with varying degrees of success in most Mexican cities. Because UPMs address issues such as housing, services, and the high cost of living—traditionally the domain of the woman as the organizer of the family's social reproduction—women constitute the majority of participants in many UPMs. As they became "vociferous and demanding" (Bennett 1992, 256), women continually battled sexism within the UPMs (Valenzuela-Arce 1991). While women outnumbered males in all of the UPMs, accounting for 80 to 85 percent of UPM participants, they were not merely underrepresented but sometimes totally absent from

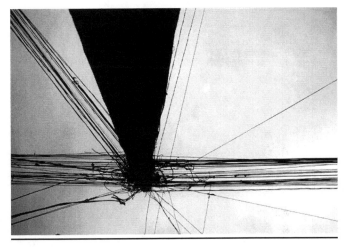

Figure 10. Connecting to power. 2005.

leadership ranks (Adler-Hellman 2008; Drukier 1995; Gonzales 2003; Haber 2006). This is where Maclovio Rojas markedly differs.

Community president Hortensia Hernández has dedicated her entire adult life to Maclovio Rojas and become a central figure in the community through her multiple reelections.[3] Her role as a leader came up repeatedly in my conversations with other women, who generally believed in and trusted her; as Dora once said to me, Hortensia is also their "political muse." Perhaps it is through her example that Hortensia has modeled the possibility of leadership—for example, through the community's expansion into five sections: Granjas (farm area), Vías (near the train tracks), Acueducto (near the aqueduct), Ampliación (the section that was added to the original township), and Poblado Viejo (old town). Each section has a coordinator who works directly with the executive committee; each coordinator in turn works with the *jefas de manzana*, or block coordinators (equivalent to a neighborhood), when organizing events and rallies or circulating information within the community. Through these organizational formations, the community is modeling participatory democracy and horizontalism. While Maclovianos/as don't name it as such, Sitrin's

(2014) definition of horizontalism aptly applies here: "The use of direct democracy and the striving for consensus, processes in which attempts are made to let everyone be heard is a new way of relating, based in affective politics and mutual empowerment."

By the time I arrived in Maclovio Rojas, the executive committee had developed a visionary community economic plan to create family farms (*granjas*), a farmer's market (*sobre-ruedas*), and roadside commercial lots (*lotes comerciales*) to autonomously support the residents and families outside of the confines of the maquiladoras and other exploitive labor. They also proposed forty-three projects including an orphanage, an Internet café, cemetery, library, and a university to the asamblea and residents. Of these projects, approximately twenty-two have been completed or initiated including the schools, childcare center, and the Aguascalientes in honor of the call made by the Zapatistas in 1996.[4] Many of the homes in Maclovio Rojas are made out of wood pallets and discarded garage doors donated or brought from the United States; newer houses are being erected out of cinderblock and mortar. After years of lacking electricity, the residents have created webs of electric lines that crisscross the streets, streaming down from the power poles that the government has installed for the maquiladoras but that are not connected to their homes; for years they tapped into an aqueduct that carries water through the middle of their neighborhood to the nearby Samsung megaplant (Mancillas 2002).

Despite the state's classification of the community as an irregular land settlement with residents simply seeking shelter for their families, Maclovio Rojas is a developing community with a vision of its future in the process of becoming fully realized through participatory planning practices and the distinct forms of autonomous self-governance that women like Hortensia have made possible. And, while the community must operate within the larger sociopolitical system of the neoliberal state, it nonetheless consciously materializes a counterhegemonic project.

Figure 11. Working together. 2005.

Figure 12. Arriving at school. 2005.

Figure 13. Sobre ruedas. Photo by Oscar Michel. 2010.

In the neighborhood Las Vías, I attended meetings where the *comerciantes* were planning their future marketplace.[5] I became friends with several of the business owners, and it was there that I met Doña Meche, Jorge, and Mari Chuy through Paula. In one conversation with Jorge I learned that he had been living in Maclovio Rojas for five years; he described his community as a community in *lucha*. He told me that what they have in Maclovio Rojas they couldn't have anywhere else. "It's sacrifice and work," he said, "and maybe in this generation we won't see the benefits but our children will." I learned of their shared sense of responsibility—not only for this generation but for those that were yet to come. This is reflected in the poblado's vision for the *cerro de esperanzas* (hill of hopes) where they plan to build a university in the future.

The Rise of Maclovio Rojas

As noted earlier, Baja California was the first Mexican state to electorally rebel against the PRI—the party in power in Mexico since 1929—in countless local and state elections, replacing it with it the PAN party in 1989 (Martinez 1988). The conservative Panistas did not offer much to the the the working-class and the poor. Quite the opposite, their win proved to be even more detrimental to border women and their families. Hortensia recalls when her father, members of CIOAC, and eighteen families, at the advice of the federal Agrarian Reform Department, squatted on the national lands where Maclovio Rojas now sits. They were under the impression that soon thereafter they would be granted the lands. But instead

> ese año fue un año de elecciones y el PAN llegó al poder entonces había un gobierno nuevo y fue cuando empezamos a tener problemas. En ese tiempo todavía era una mujer joven y estaba involucrada en la toma de tierra en el 1988.

(that year was an election year and the PAN came into office and so there was a new governor and that's when we began to have problems. At that time I was still a young woman and I was involved in the takeover of the lands in 1988).

When I listen to her tell the story of those early days, I sense great admiration for her father and a bit of nostalgia in her voice. It's not likely that the experience of Maclovianos would have been different had another political party won the governorship that year, but they did see the change in party leadership as a potential aperture for support. Their disappointment sparked a continued commitment to their community.

In 1996, soon after the election of the second Panista governor, Hector Terán Terán (1995–98), the residents of Maclovio Rojas organized La Marcha por la Libertad, as recalled by BAW/TAF artist and activist Manuel Mancillas:

Wednesday morning, September 4, 1996. The main plaza of the Poblado Maclovio Rojas was full of people. Women and children milling around, painting banners and signs, preparing their bodies and souls for the road ahead, packing food, water, and hydrolyzed serum donated by supporters. Their resolve was strong: they would march to meet face to face with the governor of Baja California. Highway 2 will take the marchers through the 5,500 feet Sierra Juarez pass, down the Rumorosa grade to the Laguna Salada 110 feet below sea level, where temperatures can climb to 115 degrees at midday. Over 300 people began the march, the corridor of power waited for no one, not even freedom marchers. The madness grew intense, impatient horns blasted through the morning sun; a massive traffic jam backed up for miles. Dirt and smoke filtered the colors flying in the sky. One marcher, Rubén Hernández died while crossing the desert. The Maclovianos pledged to return a year later to the place where he died, and erected a monument in his honor and for Freedom. (Mancillas 2001)[6]

In her research on colonias in New Mexico, Dolhinow (2006) ties the neoliberal political project to the work of the NGOs and their leadership, arguing that the empowerment projects of those organizations are self-serving and individualistic and do not lead to progressive social change. Instead, the NGOs support the neoliberal state, even if only inadvertently, by creating passive subjects. This is not the case in Maclovio Rojas, where the institutions of collective action are rebuilding the social commons, and the basis for this radical alternative is women's political subjectivity. Not to be conflated with identity, this subjectivity emerges through women's dynamic forms of emergent leadership, which tie together individual, material, and social changes in their community with profound implications for the larger border region and other similar communities across the Global South.

Political mobilization in Maclovio Rojas differs markedly from the forms of self-activity and governance promoted by transnational nongovernmental agencies and organizations (NGOs). As Dohlinow (2010) cogently argues, the NGOs think of leadership and governance in entrepreneurial terms, as an individualistic self-serving enterprise that relieves the state of responsibility for supporting everyone by allowing the most organized sectors of the poor to make gains at the expense of the unorganized. In contrast, the ideals of empowerment, following Cruikshank's (1999) notion of power (which recognizes people's potentialities as always existing, not through assumption of powerlessness), that have emerged from the struggles of Maclovio Rojas revolve around a model of solidarity and collectivity that points the way toward progressive social change for society as a whole—that is, a commitment to organizing the unorganized in the process of uplifting everyone. Through challenging corporations, governments, and transnational agencies and institutions, this autonomous activism generates new social subjects and subjectivities as well as new identities and new identifications. The women-centered political subjectivity that guides this not only produces new individual leaders, but also new understandings of leadership as collective, transformative, and accountable, giving Maclovianas control of their "collective ability to imagine new possibilities" (Mora 2003, 26).

I do heed Abu-Lughod's (1990) caution against misattributing forms of consciousness or romanticizing politics. Viewing empowerment through the collective raising of consciousness is one of the practices that can lead to personal and societal transformation (Delgado-Gaitán 1993). These forms of community-building place the locus of change not solely at the institutional and social level, but also in personal and collective transformation and struggle.

Late one evening, I sat in on an *asamblea* held in the Aguascalientes. I watched as the leaders tried to get support for the coming march that would begin at the nearby shopping center and end at the the governor's palace, which houses the offices of CESPT. I observed the tired faces of the approximately thirty residents crowded together in the office: mothers sat with their children falling asleep in their arms. One of the organizers, Dora, asked who was going to be able to make it; no one raised a hand. After a few moments of silence, Rosa, the daughter of Nicolasa, who was going on her second year of incarceration (for the alleged "theft" of water), stood up. Through tears, she cried,

¿Qué les pasa? Yo sé que estamos cansados, yo sé que queremos tranquilidad. Pero por favor, no se desanimen. Son casi dos años sin que no he podido estar con mi mamá. Sin que mi hijita ha podido jugar con su abuela. ¡Piensen en ella! ¡Ella está pagando por el "robo de agua," pero todos los usamos! No nos dejen solos por favor, no nos abandonen.

(What is going on? I know we are tired, I know we want peace. But please don't give up. It's been two years since I've been with my mother. Since my little daughter has played with her grandmother. Think of her! She is paying for the "theft of water," but we all use it! Please don't leave us alone, don't abandon us.)

Dora reminded the residents in attendance that "Podría haber sido cualquier de nosotros" (It could've been any one of us) that was arrested for the communal use of the water.

The residents mumbled in agreement and started to shift around in their chairs, and soon an elderly man stood up to express his support. Before my eyes I witnessed the weariness in their faces replaced with a spark, or *chispa*, as Coronado (2006) describes in her work of women activists along the U.S.-Mexico border. Through their lived experience they understood the injustice of Nicolasa's incarceration, and they knew their struggle had not yet been won. Everyone promised to go back to their blocks to ensure participation from their neighbors. As Forbis (2006) highlights, the community assembly becomes a place to find transformative justice and accountability.

I looked over at the sign on the community board that read: "El lema del gobierno es: divide y vencerás y el de Maclovio es: la unión hace la fuerza porque lo hemos demostrado por más de 15 años de lucha" (The motto of the government is: divide and conquer and the one in Maclovio: unity gives strength and we have demonstrated that for over 15 years of struggle). And it is to this collective strength, identity, and unity that connects the coming chapters. In recent years, the community has obtained a legal supply of electricity. They already pay for water, although the municipal service uses the installation made by the residents (Zulaica 2015).

When the leaders remind the residents, "Lo que tenemos lo tenemos por nosotros" (What we have, we have because of ourselves), they are reinforcing an ethos of collective resistance grounded not only in a shared history but a shared vision for a shared future, as well as a recognition that if they don't, no one else will. In some ways they do not focus on an outcome as the measure of success, but rather on the internal and personal transformation of individuals who together create a community. This leads to a personal sense of dignity, community, and power, which can lead to action and, ultimately, to change.

Gendered Subjectivities: "Fe-en-mi-misma," or Having Faith in Myself

When the community leaders and residents of Maclovio Rojas stood up to the Hyundai Corporation in 1990, they likely never imagined the battle that lay ahead of them. But the residents' investment in their community grew as the settlement expanded. During one of the asambleas I attended in the fall of 2004, the education committee, led by Doña Maria, proposed the building of a new school. Since the community had grown so much, the children from the western part of the community found it difficult to commute. In the meeting, community members decided to build a second elementary school. Over the next several months, I watched as the residents constructed four wooden frames for classrooms and helped bring in materials for teaching. Initially, parents and community leaders taught the classes, but, eventually, in order for their children to receive state recognition of their education, state-employed teachers were designated, whose lack of enthusiasm and low commitment to the community were duly noted. These teachers, early in their careers, seemed to see themselves as paying dues before being sent off to teach at better schools in the city. Consequently, residents appealed to the State Department of Education for better support and construction materials. In response, the community received a dilapidated school bus and was told that it could be used as a fifth classroom. Since the bus retained heat and magnified the tropical sunshine, students were constantly uncomfortable, thirsty, and unable to learn. Residents were furious.

This example marks the countless ways in which the State consistently denies Maclovianas/os their rights, while also revealing moments of creative resistance and thriving. Blackwell's (2006) study of Indigenous women activists in Mexico demonstrates their development of a strategy of weaving between local, national, and transnational scales of power to create new spaces of participation as well as new forms of consciousness, identity, and discourse. Similarly, the narratives of the Maclovianas speak to the emergence of a woman's political subjectivity that gives them the ability to act in multiple spaces. Initially, the women came to Maclovio Rojas in search of land and shelter, but through their engagements with the State—especially its denial of public services and direct assaults against their growing community—they discovered both their own agency and the ability to affect change while expanding the meanings of land and shelter. This subjectivity allows Maclovianas to connect and simultaneously critique the State, transnational companies, and their experiences of subjugation within the home.

Women have been instrumental to the organization of protests, taking over the highway and holding vigils on their land when threats of invasion grew near. Yet the majority of women have also managed their homes without the support of their male partners and have often suffered abuse. By critically examining the conditions of their lives vis-à-vis the State, the women also began to similarly examine the conditions of their home lives. Just as shared experiences with the class system in Mexico led them to become residents of an autonomous community, their linked fate as women has made it necessary for them to confront domestic violence. Through their constant interaction with one another, moreover, the women created a supportive environment to discuss issues of emotional and physical abuse.

I recall the moment when Maria was being abused by her husband, and we all ran to her home to assist her. Afterward, we all walked back to the office together, and nobody immediately left; we all remained to process what had just happened and to discuss ways in which we could support her. Perhaps my being there created an opportunity for dialogue, or maybe it forced it. I know Maria was embarrassed, but, by engaging together in thoughtful dialogue, we understood that this moment of shared experience and collective struggle can create a transformative space. In this way, women like Maria begin to imagine alternatives and, in turn, leave their abusive home environments, evidencing a dialectical relationship between private life and public activism. In the process of changing society, they are changing themselves, their communities, and their relationship to each other.

Diaz-Barriga (1998) analyzes the contested terrain of the domestic and public spheres in women's activism by applying the borderlands concept of existing in a state of "in-betweeness" to reveal how women activists deploy a variety of strategies to identify practical gender-based needs that blur distinctions between the domestic and public spheres. Borrowing from both Anzaldúa (1987) and Rosaldo (1989), theorists who highlight the creative ways in which social actors navigate the intersections of social experience, Diaz-Barriga underscores the way women's involvement resists the relegation of either domestic or public life to separate incommensurable spheres of existence.

Feminist scholarship (e.g., Aguilar and Chenard 1994; Bennett 1992; Corcoran-Nantes 2003; Pardo 1998; Safa 1990; Stephen 2003) challenges the binary oppositions between public and private spheres and generally points to women's experiences as mothers and wives as the key experiences that shape the roles they take on as public activists. However, Dolhinow (2006) has found that women who emerge as leaders are either single or in "unusually" egalitarian relationships. To the contrary, what I found in Maclovio Rojas is that the point of departure for women activists is *not* interpersonal relations within the home. Rather, through their political and personal relationships with other women leaders in the community, their woman-centered political subjectivity and consciousness develop, and the women respond in ways that are constitutive of and reinforce their newfound sense of self. The spaces of women's collective struggle in Maclovio Rojas are not contained in either the public or private sphere. The activism of these women challenges traditional gender roles in both spheres simultaneously.

The borderlands concept—or in-betweenness subjectivity— highlights how Maclovianas, through their bridging of experiences as land squatters, activists, wives, and mothers, are transforming social relations and perhaps cultural meanings as well. This in-betweenness also helps show how the lives of the residents challenge interpersonal violence. The new subjectivity forged by the Maclovianas is similar to Sandoval's (2000) notion of a tactical subjectivity that posits the capacity to "de- and recenter, given the forms of power to be moved" (59). As they battle transnational corporations, the State, and domestic abuse, the Maclovianas create new identities, identifications, and imaginaries.

Active Actors Against the Neoliberal State

When families first squatted on the land now known as Maclovio Rojas, it was vacant for miles around. Those initial squatters often described to me how beautiful it had been then, especially seeing the vast, barren land and the mountains on the horizon. In the course of the last thirty years, however, all of that has dramatically changed. The community sits in the middle of an ever-expanding industrial park. The Hyundai Corporation owns massive rows of trailers that brush up against the community; both the Samsung and Coca-Cola factories are visible. As a result of this rapid commercial expansion, the surrounding areas are becoming more populated with government-subsidized housing that Hortensia and other residents say is overpriced, much too small, and ugly. The highway that connects the city of Tijuana with the city of Tecate runs just past the community, which means ubiquitous heavy traffic of trailer trucks to transport imports, exports, and shared goods between the Mexican cities and across the border. At the beginning of my fieldwork, plans were already under way to implement the Tijuana Boulevard 2000, which would have stretched just beyond the community's Via section and put an expressway *inside* the community.[7] Unbeknownst to them, the original residents had landed unintentionally on prime real estate at an important time due to the shifting plans of the neoliberal state and its central role in the global economy. Furthermore, their resistance in holding on to their land defies the interests of both the State and transnational companies. In other words, Maclovianas are in the way. For the first twenty years, standoffs occurred between local law enforcement officers and the residents. State officials thought that they could use brute force to remove the residents, but they did not count on the resiliency of the women who were willing to hold vigils on their land in protest, nor did state officials count on the number of strategic interventions that the community collectively came together to enact.

Luz deeply understands the value of the Maclovio Rojas land: "Hay muchos intereses que el gobierno tiene aquí. La tierra tiene mucho valor así que tenemos más problemas con ellos porque quieren construir casas o maquilas aquí" (There are a lot of interests that the government has here. The lands have a lot of value so we have more problems with them because they want to build housing or factories here). In 1998, local police forcibly tried to take over the homes of several residents. As the inhabitants defended their homes with their bodies, other residents began dragging furniture onto the highway, blocking traffic and directly effecting the companies that use the highway to transport goods, which caused the police to back off. Instances such as these have been common for Maclovio Rojas residents. Teresa concludes, "Hemos tenido peleas, luchas. . . . no le costaría mucho al gobierno venir y golpearnos" (We've had some fights, some struggles. . . . It wouldn't cost the government much to come and beat us up).

Residents are well aware of the fate of another UPM in Baja California: Puertos al Futuro. In the summer of 2002, the Tijuana municipal government carried out a very controversial program of destroying substandard, irregular housing. Between 250 and 300 houses were demolished in Puertos al Futuro, leaving more than 500 people homeless (Kopinak, 2003). However, because physical threats of removal did not completely deter land movements in Baja California, Article

226 was introduced to the state penal code in 2002, which made land occupation illegal (*despojo*). When a community resident or leader is charged with despojo, an arrest warrant is immediately sought. It is important to note the judicial system in Mexico works on the principle that one is guilty until proven innocent; if a claim is made against an individual, and they have not sought an *amparo* (which is almost like a bond, but literally means "protection of a right"), they are subject to immediate arrest. Sometimes amparos are not allowed, and defendants, if caught, have to wait in jail until their case is resolved. CESPT also filed charges against residents for the alleged theft of untreated water from the aqueduct. At one point, there were over forty-two charges of despojo against several residents. Some leaders were targeted in multiple cases, creating chaos as the accused scrambled to and from court appearances and meetings with lawyers.

The disruptive cycle of these lawsuits creates an insidious but subtle wave of repression, not only through the creation of fear, but also by disturbing the everyday lives of those that have been charged. For example, on one of my many visits to the courthouse, the plaintiff (in this particular case it was CESPT) did not show up to the hearing, and all fourteen residents who came to the hearing wasted yet another day of their lives. Furthermore, these lawsuits have served as a justification for sending troops into the Maclovio Rojas community to arrest leaders and cause general intimidation. The residents refer to these as *golpes*—essentially an attempted overthrow. The biggest golpe to the community came in 2002, driving two prominent leaders, Artemio and Hortensia, into hiding and landing two others, Juan and Nicolasa, in jail.[8]

The golpe of 2002 is critical to the community's historical memory—more so, of course, for Hortensia, whose visible leadership has made her the target of multiple attacks from the government. She has felt the brunt of repression personally, in the form of arrest warrants, persecution, and imprisonment. Governmental tactics are not hidden, as Hortensia clearly explained:

El gobierno no puede hacer lo que hizo en Puertos al Futuro . . . ya lo intentaron, la última vez fue en el 1998 y llegaron los tractores y todo . . . la gente lo opuso y se pusieron en frente de las máquinas y defendieron sus tierras contra la policía. Ellos saben que nos vamos a defender y van a haber muertes, asi que mejor sutilmente quieren tomar el poder con demandas.

(The government can't do what they did in Puertos al Futuro . . . they already tried, the last time was in 1998 and the tractors came and everything . . . the people opposed it and put themselves in front of the machines and defended their lands against the police. They know we will defend ourselves and there will be deaths, so instead they subtly take power through lawsuits.)

The repression and the battles that have ensued have engendered an oppositional stance against the government. As Teresa explained, "Con todo lo que vives, le empiezas a tener más amor a lo que tienes, y te enojas con el gobierno. Queremos pelear por nuestro pedazo de tierra en donde podemos vivir y alimentarnos" (With everything that you live, you start having more love for what you have, and you get angry with the government. We want to fight for our piece of land where we can live and feed ourselves). Alma articulated a critique of the government:

Hay muchas injusticias, y hay mucho que se dice que son puras mentiras, porque he estado cerca de los líderes [del gobierno] y puedo ver que es verdad que manejan las cosas y personas con mentiras. Mucha gente no tiene líderes que los guíe y cuando te das cuenta de las cosas que pasan, sólo dices que no, lo único que quieren [el gobierno] es vivir a gusto robando, y aquí en Maclovio Rojas, no lo permitimos, y por eso con mas ganas están en contra de nosotros . . . el gobierno vende las tierras y luego reclama su derecho legítimo de la propiedad y luego corre a los dueños. Lo han hecho en varios lugares, y eso no es justo. En Maclovio Rojas no lo hemos permitido, y eso es la lucha.

(There are a lot of injustices, and there's a lot that is said that are just lies, because I've been close to the leaders [of the government] and I can see that it is true that they run things and people with lies. Many people don't have [community] leaders to guide them, and when you become aware of the things that happen, you just say no, all they [the government] want to do is live comfortably by stealing, and here in Maclovio Rojas, we don't allow it, and that's why they are against us with more motivation . . . the government sells lands and then claims rightful ownership of it and then drives out the people who own it. They've done this in various places, and that is unjust. In Maclovio Rojas we haven't allowed it, and that's the struggle.)

Because the community is surrounded by a large industrial park, it is not surprising that the maquiladoras also "illegally" tapped into the aqueduct. Yet no lawsuits have been filed against them. Hortensia asserted:

Hay millones de dólares en juego. Estamos en un punto estratégico donde el Boulevard 2000—un autopista que facilitará el camino de camiones de carga cruzando el estado—va a pasar y el interés de las compañías transnacionales esta allí. Como somos una comunidad organizada, servimos como mal ejemplo porque podríamos despertar la conciencia de la gente.

(There are millions of dollars at stake. We are in a strategic point where the Boulevard 2000—a highway that will ease the way for cargo trucks across the state—is going to pass and the interests of the transnational companies are there. Since we are an organized community, we serve as a bad example because we might wake the consciousness of the people.)

By using the term "bad," Hortensia is recognizing that the movement in Maclovio Rojas is an insurgent one that would bring a political consciousness beyond Maclovianos—one that the state and local
government are consistently trying to negate.

Whereas the colonias of Dolhinow's study were led and managed
by leaders from without, in the form of NGOs, the leadership in
Maclovio Rojas comes from within. Dolhinow (2006) does make a
compelling argument about the ways in which leaders in the colonias and the NGOs that serve them work together to fill in the gap
where the State and capital are no longer securing the basics of social
reproduction. But this argument does not account for longer historical pattern of neglect that is closely related to contemporary neoliberal politics and derives directly from colonialism and conquest:
the marginalization has always existed with women most targeted.
Furthermore, it assumes that the State once did observe these responsibilities. This simply hasn't been the case in Mexico, much less in the
northern border region.

The consciousness of the residents of Maclovio Rojas has already
been awakened. Maclovianas did not have a critique of the State prior
to their involvement with the struggle for land. Through their collective engagement, a new political consciousness emerged and, corre-
spondingly, a new subjectivity. When forced to confront the structural
violence endemic to the border region, residents point to an alternative
that challenges the gendered and racialized sociopolitical positions in
which they find themselves. Arguably, the residents of Maclovio Rojas
came together initially because they simply needed a place to live and
through this experience came to an understanding that the State *would
not* provide for them. The women described at length the hardships of
migration, instability, and uncertainty they endured before settling on
these lands. Upon arriving and finding the neoliberal state resistant to
their rights to the land, however, the women emerged as leaders, and
they fought back. Over the years, it became clear that resolving their
problems requires them to take it upon themselves to find solutions.

Through this process, the women fashioned a critique of the transnational companies that employ them, as well as of the State. The women immediately understand that the State wants to see them removed—their bodies relocated—so that the transnational companies can have access to their land. Seeing themselves as political subjects accompanied their self-recognition that they have the power to enact change. Hortensia stated, "Mire mi caso. A mi me persiguen por ser luchadora de justicia social cuando el gobierno me debe de entregar el respeto como ciudadana, esposa, hija; me están quitando mis derechos" (Look at my case. I'm being persecuted for being a social justice fighter when I should be given respect from the government as a citizen, wife, daughter; they are taking away my rights). As a result of this consciousness and the desire for respect across multiple dimensions of their lives, the Maclovianas begin to challenge the conditions of their interpersonal relationships, creating safer spaces and more dignified treatment in every aspect of their lives.

Transforming the Home

Elizabeth is one of the community's original residents. Prior to arriving in Maclovio Rojas, she, her husband, and their children struggled for many years to find shelter. She resides in the Poblado Viejo and lives in a humble home: one large room for the kitchen, a living room, a dining area, and two smaller bedrooms. Early in our conversation, I found out that her husband had passed away a couple of years before. Yet it was not until the end of the day that her tragic story came together, when I started noticing things like his name crossed out on the door, the absence of his pictures in the house, the way she did not mention his name. Her husband, I came to find out, was emotionally, physically, and sexually abusive to her. He had temporarily stopped the abuse when he became a Jehovah's Witness, but then he left the church and, after twenty years of marriage, told Elizabeth that he was leaving her for her best friend, a *compañera* from the community.[9] Her husband and friend both left the community. Devastated, Elizabeth focused her energies on community projects and when he tried reconciling with her several weeks later, she did not allow him back. Two months later, he hanged himself from a tree.

Countless studies have shown that Mexico's legal system ratifies and promotes violence against women, especially in the private sphere, where male violence is normalized as "a mechanism of punishment and control" (Fregoso 2007, 51). Furthermore, the State tolerates this violence, depoliticizing and trivializing it as a private matter (INCITE! 2006; Menjivar 2011; Olivera 2010). Reinforcing these manifestations of family violence is a discourse that discourages women from leaving the private sphere, the purported site of patriarchal protection and authority; public space is imagined as inherently dangerous (Fregoso 2007). As Speed, Hernandez Castillo, and Stephen (2006) argue, "Family structure works as a contradictory core: it is simultaneously a unit of solidarity and resistance which implements cooperative strategies for survival and reproduction, and a power structure which establishes the internal relations and women's place within them where inequality is marked by gender and generation" (80). This process produces a unique combination of domestic centrality and economic marginality that ensures male advantage supported by women's captive labor and child-rearing in the home while disadvantaging women by limiting their access to public sphere politics.

Yet, as these women solidify their commitment to the struggle for their land in Maclovio Rojas, they also commit themselves to a life ethic that demands justice in all aspects of their lives. There is a well-known *dicho* (saying) in Maclovio Rojas: "Si una mujer llega a Maclovio Rojas casada, se divorcia, y si llega soltera encuentra pareja" (If a woman comes to Maclovio Rojas married, she divorces, and if she arrives single she will find a partner). This notion illustrates the discord in traditional family life that occurs when women develop political consciousness through their critical engagement against the State and transnational companies. This becomes most apparent when the women negotiate their lived experiences of violence within the home. Of the ten women I interviewed, five made the decision to leave their partners based on their experiences of violence and humiliation. All argue that becoming more deeply involved in the movement created schisms within their homes. Accusations of infidelity were common as women attended marches, rallies, and meetings. The women argue, however, that *being* involved in the movement allowed them to *see* that they did not have to remain in their violent situation at home.

This borderlands subjectivity highlights important aspects of the process in which both the private and public spheres become politicized spaces for the women. As Maria states:

Yo tenía problemas con mi esposo. Él sentía que había abandonado mi hogar, nuestros hijos, mis responsabilidades con ellos. Siempre andaba negativo porque nunca entendió la lucha, y digo nunca porque hemos estado separados por cuatro meses y hasta se fue de la comunidad sin entender lo que estaba pasando, o el trabajo que hago. Se fue hablando mal de la comunidad, la organización, diciendo que por la organización perdió su familia; por la organización perdió todo. Yo digo que es fácil de entender porque hasta mi hijo menor entiende y vive esta experiencia conmigo y él quiere apoyar algo que mi esposo no quiso.

(I was having problems with my husband. He felt that I had abandoned our home, our children, my responsibilities with them. He was always negative because he never understood the *lucha*, and I say never because we've been separated now for four months and he went as far as to leave the community never really understanding what was going on, or the work that I do. He left talking bad about the community, the organization, saying that because of the organization he lost his family; because of the organization he lost it all. I say that it's easy to understand because even my youngest son understands and lives this experience with me and he wants to support something that my husband didn't want to.)

Maria made the decision to separate from her husband and chose, instead, to continue her work within the movement:

Al final, pues, quizás puedes decir que fue una mala decisión pero mis valores no me dejaban ir, sensaciones de responsabilidad y solidaridad . . . y yo no quise abandonar a la organización en un momento tan crítico. Además de ser miembra de la organización, soy miembra de la comunidad. Tengo propiedad aquí así que mi obligación es apoyar el movimiento. Si yo me hubiera ido, mi conciencia no me hubiera dejado en paz. Yo sabía que no era el momento. Si no lo hice antes cuando quizás podría haber salvado mi matrimonio, pues más tarde no era el momento apropiado para irme. Ya estaba demasiada involucrada . . . ya no me estreso tanto porque la actitud de mi esposo siempre me afectaba negativamente. La manera que me hablaba interrumpía mis ideas, y ahora que estoy sola con los niños, es mejor. Ellos entienden que si hay una reunión o si hay una protesta es mi obligación a la comunidad . . . ellos entienden que en ese momento no puedo estar con ellos.

(In the end, well, perhaps you can say that it was a bad decision but my values wouldn't let me leave, feelings of responsibility and solidarity . . . and I didn't want to abandon the organization at such a critical time. Besides being a member of the organization, I am a community member. I have property here and so my obligation is to support the movement. If I had left, my conscience wouldn't have let me be in peace. I knew it wasn't the time. If I didn't do it earlier when maybe it could've saved my marriage, then later just wasn't the appropriate time to leave. I was too deeply involved . . . I no longer get as stressed out because my husband's attitude always affected me negatively. The way he was speaking to me interrupted my thoughts, and now that I'm alone with the kids, it's better. They understand that if there is a meeting or if there's a protest it's my obligation to the community . . . they understand that at that moment I can't be with them.)

Maria describes the tensions felt in her relationships with her children, husband, and the movement. Her sense of obligation to all three areas of her life never waned. What she articulates is that she needed reciprocity in all three relationships, which she was able to receive from her young children and members of her community. But her husband not only failed to support her; he responded with increased violence. Maria was the community leader for whom I was asked to intervene at the beginning of my field research. Once Maria made the decision to leave her husband, she never looked back.

Although the Maclovianas admit that their experiences have been painful, they also describe the process of coming to consciousness as a liberating one, that the movement helped them "open their minds." Juana detailed:

Nos estamos enfrentando al gobierno y es algo grande, no es cualquier cosa, y yo creo que eso te da más fuerza. Hasta si no quieres, porque antes no me interesaba. Pero ahora, estando involucrada en el movimiento, te influye porque ves al gobierno cometiendo tantas injusticias, como desigualdad de salarios y eso. Pasan por encima de la gente! Aquí sólo estamos tratando de avanzar por nuestras familias . . . y uno empieza a darse cuenta al involucrarse más y como mujeres no podemos permitir esto y nuestras mentes empiezan a abrirse. Cuando empiezas a entender más, allí es donde empieza nuestra libertad. Maclovio nos ha ayudado a avanzarnos, enfrentar nuevos desafíos, metas y obstáculos. Hemos avanzado poco y mucho. Tenemos que deshacernos de la barrera del machismo.

(We're confronting the government and it's a huge thing, it's no small feat, and I think that gives you more strength. Even if you don't want to, because before it didn't interest me. But now, being involved in the movement, it influences you because you see the government committing so many injustices, such as salary inequalities and such. They run all over people! Here we're just trying to get ahead for our families . . . and one starts realizing more as you get more involved and as women we cannot permit this and our minds start to open up. When you start understanding more, then that's where our freedom starts. Maclovio has helped us to move forward, to face new challenges, goals and obstacles. We have advanced both a little bit and a lot. We need to do away with the barrier of machismo.)

Despite her disinterest in politics when she first became involved with the land struggle, Juana, through her experiences, can now articulate a critique of the State and recognizes the injustices imposed on workers and on the poor in general. When given the opportunity to develop a critique of the State in relation to their place in the social world, the women begin to critically examine their own lives. As they draw connections between the forms of violence imposed by the State and those endured in the home, their new political consciousness creates a fury that motivates them to act more "freely" and without fear. By bridging their experiences as land squatters, residents, activists, wives, and mothers, Maclovianas are transforming social relations. Multiple layers of women's lives contribute to their political consciousness. Juana says, "Antes le tenía miedo a mi esposo y poco a poco me empecé a defender; no lo vas a creer, pero del primer hijo al siguiente no tengo el mismo miedo" (Before I was scared of my husband and little by little I started defending myself; you're not going to believe it, but from my first child to the next I don't have the same fear). This is the way that Juana discovered her freedom.

Women who were more actively involved in the movement and made the decision to split from their partners were the ones who then created safe spaces to support each other financially and emotionally, as well as with child-rearing. While victimization, abuse, and, in the case of two women, death at the hands of their live-in partners all still occur in Maclovio Rojas, mechanisms now in place there demonstrate that women's roles are being reconsidered. As noted, single women are given priority for land, and wives and mothers given official titles to it, a practice that is uncommon in Mexico. Furthermore, the women's center, Casa de la Mujer, provides childcare and workshops on reproductive rights, skill building, and creative outlets for women residents of Maclovio Rojas, valuing the labor that women perform inside and outside of home and giving the support that working mothers need. A statue of Coatlique—the Mesoamerican goddess of life, death, and rebirth—stands in the front of the center, a symbolic homage to women and their needs that only such a center can fulfill. As Juana summarized, "Todas las que trabjamos aquí y apoyando somos mujeres y te sientes más segura en ti misma ya que no necesitas tanto de tu pareja sabes que tú lo puedes hacer sola" (All of us that are working and supporting here are women, and it gives you security about yourself that you don't need much from your partner so that you can make it on your own).

Despite these important gains, leaders identify considerable limitations to further development of the Casa de la Mujer because their energies are consumed with the immediate struggle for land. While woman-centered vision exists, leaders have not been able to articulate and put into action an intersectional analysis of needs that places equal importance on the evolution of the Casa de la Mujer as they have with fighting for legal recognition of their lands and homes. Clearly the issues are interrelated, but the connection— and, perhaps, the necessary "buy-in"—has not been made within the entire community. Therefore, women are still responsible for the tasks accorded to them historically, including housework and child-rearing. While in Maclovio Rojas women are the defenders of homes (in fact, they are the ones who attend the rallies, the marches,

Figure 14. Casa de la Mujer. 2005.

Figure 15. Day care center. Photo by Oscar Michel. 2010.

Figure 16. "Coatlicue" by Efrain Greco-Novelo, sculpture in front of the Casa de la Mujer. Photo by Oscar Michel. 2010.

and the protests and also confront the police or other invaders if necessary), this gendered historical prototype has not changed. Nonetheless, Elizabeth acknowledges that despite the tragedy of her circumstance having the space of the Casa de la Mujer and access to workshops—and the mutual support from other residents—has given her the foundation she has needed to navigate the future for herself and her daughters.

Rethinking Feminism and Faith

Although an express call to feminism has not been made (indeed, I never once heard the women—not even the leaders—use *feminista* as a descriptor for themselves), their actions demonstrate a woman-centered subjectivity that has been engendered by their experiences. This is similar to Milagros Peña's (2007) concept of "fe-en-mi-misma" in her work on women's NGOs in El Paso/Ciudad Juárez, where the activists defined feminism as having faith in themselves. Maclovianas feel that they have become *otra* (other), stronger women, and feel that because of their ability to defend their homes they can defend themselves in their personal lives as well. Paula stated:

> He aprendido defenderme para que ellos [el gobierno] no se lleven lo que es nuestro. Estas tierra son mías y sólo porque el gobierno las quiera no quiere decir que me las puedan quitar. Yo las voy a defender porque yo valoro todo lo que tengo aquí.

> (I've learned to defend myself so that they [the government] don't take what is ours. These lands are mine and just because the government wants them doesn't mean they can take them away from me. I will defend them because I value everything that I have here.)

Teresa identified what she had learned:

Ser más valiente. Ya no le temo al gobierno. Yo me puedo defender
porque al principio sí te da miedo pero con el paso del tiempo aprendes
más. Le tienes más amor a lo que tienes y hasta te hace enojar más. Me
hace sentir bien ayudar a mi comunidad.

(To be more courageous. I'm not scared of the government anymore.
I can defend myself because in the beginning it scares you but with
the passage of time you learn more. You have more love towards what
you have and it makes you get more mad. It makes me feel good to
help my community.)

Maria talked about what she has learned most from living and
working in the community:

Antes le tenía mucho miedo a Juan pero ya no. Ahora sé como
enfrentármelo. No sólo soy representante de la comunidad, pero soy
responsable de mis hijos, y su seguridad siempre es primero. Eso quiere decir que no le puedo tener miedo a nada. Tengo que tener más
confianza en mi misma.

(Before I used to be very scared of Juan but I'm not anymore. I know
how to confront him now. Not only am I a representative of the community, but I am responsible for my children, and their security is
always first. So that means that I can't be scared of anything. I have to
have more confidence in myself.)

Juana shared what she values most in Maclovio Rojas:

He conseguido mucha confianza estando aquí, mucha confianza en mi
misma. Yo sola valerme por mí misma con mis hijos, y he aprendido
que yo sola puedo salir adelante. Si yo hubiera vivido en otra comunidad, no hubiera participado en plantones y marchas, etc. . . . En otro
lugar, esto no pasaría.

(I've gained a lot of confidence being here, a lot of confidence in myself. To be self-reliant with my children, and I have learned that by myself I can get ahead. If I would have lived in another community, I wouldn't have participated in sit-ins and marches, etc. . . . In another place, this wouldn't happen.)

Through their empowerment and "fe-en-mi-misma," feminist visions can indeed begin developing. For many Maclovianas, the journey to own a little plot of land has been a long and arduous one, and the struggle is certainly not over. But, as I have shown in this chapter, when mujeres fronterizas face the kind of gendered, class-based, and racialized structural violence endemic to the border region, they respond with what can be described as a gut instinct for survival, which leads to a political, social, cultural praxis of communal autonomy and self-reliance. Through their experiences, the women develop an oppositional consciousness that critiques the neoliberal state while simultaneously—especially for those more involved in the movement—developing a woman-centered subjectivity that provides them with the tools they need to create different choices and lives for themselves. Central to this is the ability to believe in themselves.

Understanding the specificity of a borderlands subjectivity illuminates the ways in which Maclovianas navigate these social spheres and helps to further illuminate and problematize the dichotomous notions about the public and private spheres in Chicana/Latina/Mexicana activism. Diaz-Barriga (1998) argues that women activists blur the distinction between the domestic and the public spheres. My analysis of the narratives of the women from Maclovio Rojas builds on Pardo's (1998) study, in which she emphasizes that political participation relies on the relationship between the public and the private spheres. Maclovianas direct their actions *simultaneously* at the neoliberal state and at the unequal relationships women experience within their homes, both being sociopolitical structures that condone violence. Maclovianas do not seek liberation from the private sphere as such; in fact, they are defending their homes and themselves. In this regard, their liberation comes from transforming the social relations and the cultural meanings attached to them.

CHAPTER 4

Maclovianas and the Shaping of Autonomy in the Spaces of Neoliberal Neglect

Es nuestra responsabilidad como líderes a recordarlos diario porque los gobiernos internacionales, nacionales y del estado están trabajando diario y estamos luchando en contra de todo eso. Cuando estás a solas es difícil.

(It's our responsibility as leaders to remind them daily because the international, national, and state governments are working daily and we are fighting against all of that. When you're on your own it's hard.)

—HORTENSIA HERNÁNDEZ

Autonomy from Below and in Between

MANY MANIFESTATIONS OF RESISTANCE TO neoliberal policies, global economic policies, and the world system have emerged through what Starr and Adams (2003) have termed "anti-globalization" efforts, including radical reform movements, "people's globalization," and struggles for autonomous communities. Some scholars have adopted the term "alter-globalization" to refer to the phenomenon of alternative transnational movements seeking to challenge the hegemony of neoliberalism (Pleyers 2011). Pleyers is among those who pays tribute to the Zapatistas as the source of alter-globalization movements; in a very real sense the local has gone global, but still remains local in the country of origin. Gago (2017) uses "neoliberalism from below" to describe popular attempts to resist and reformulate neoliberalism beyond its articulation as a set of policies from above as structural adjustment. Starr and Adams explain that autonomy is a particularly viable alternative to global market policies as it articulates the pleasures, productivities, and rights of communities. Esteva and Prakash (1998) agree that emerging social movements are continually searching for their liberation from the neoliberal power being imposed on them and they argue that local autonomy is the only available antidote for the "global project."

Examples in the new millenium include the Indigenous peoples in Bolivia who blocked the privatization of their water supply by a U.S. corporation, Bechtel, in a struggle that resulted in the famous Cochabamba Declaration, establishing a human and ecological right to water (Starr and Adams 2003). In Brazil, the movement of rural landless workers (MST) won land for over 250,000 families (Wolford 2004) and has been associated with the rise of La Via Campesina, a global movement of local farmer organizations organizing for what they call "food sovereignty" (Mares and Peña 2010, 2011). In Argentina, following the economic crisis of 2001, factories were taken over and run by the workers, five governments were ousted in a matter of days, and hundreds of thousands of people took to the streets (Sitrin 2012). In Monkey Point, Nicaragua, gendered activism and a community-based movement for autonomous rights that began in the late 1990s became a self-governing territory in 2009 (Goett 2016).

In Mexico, the powerful debtors' movement emerging in the mid-nineties, El Barzón, consisted of a nation-wide group of indebted small farmers and entrepreneurs. Members of El Barzón were liable for massive amounts of dollar-denominated debt, which they were expected to pay back with a peso worth half of its previous value. In a stark example of neocolonial banking, their debts would have amounted to ten times the loans they had originally taken out. Through El Barzón, elements of the traditionally "quiet" middle class rose up and refused to pay the monstrous sums of money that were expected from them by lending institutions (Chávez 1998). This action, sustained by grassroots organizations, shook up the political and economic system in Mexico, alarming the banking and finance powerhouses north and south of the border. Here I am highlighting how local struggles—steeped in the experiences, norms, and values of the local, national, or regional culture—can globalize organizational forms and terrains of struggle in a manner that is much more complex than the presumption of a two-directional process of globalized cultural and ideological interpellation largely controlled by neoliberal elites.

In this chapter, I argue that Maclovio Rojas is another example of the power of collective action against the will, logic, and policies of neoliberalism, which seeks not just to privatize life but to end politics, except as the right to individual action and self-care. These local mobilizations are redefining the political actors of the world and demonstrating how globalization from above can be challenged by a globalization from below and in-between—or in the *grietas* (cracks), as the Zapatistas point out. Oppositional impulses and communities of resistance disrupt the collaboration between states and the main agents of capital formation (Brecher, Child, and Cutler 1993). In self-determining the future of their poblado, Maclovianas/os are demanding recognition but also moving forward in developing their community according to collective goals and without the approval of the State.[1]

La Necesidad de Autonomía

One afternoon Dora said to me, "El gobierno no quiere que otras comunidades sepan, por ejemplo, que ellos también se pueden organizar. ¿Para qué necesitaríamos gobernadores o presidentes si la gente se juntaría para organizarse?" (The government doesn't want other communities to know, for example, that they too can organize themselves. What would we need governors or presidents for if the people came together to organize?) Dora's statement reflects the sentiment of the leadership—and many of the residents—in Maclovio Rojas while also raising important questions about how Maclovianas/os negotiate their relationship to the State and to each other.

Here, they make claims to their Mexican citizenship as well as recognize their community as autonomous and extol their unity among themselves. This complex sentiment is similar to Smith's (2003) description of the role of citizenship for migrants in the United States: "Membership describes the broader relations and practices of belonging and participation in a political community" (303). In other words, membership exists by virtue of participation; relationships and practices are formed that create a sense of belonging to a political community irrespective of formal government recognition. Schmidt Camacho's (2008) concept of "migrant imaginaries" captures the formation of Mexicans as a transborder laboring class who through their experience "articulate[d] expansive definitions of civic life and community that defied conventions of national citizenship in both Mexico and the United States" (9). This is also true for the residents of Maclovio Rojas, where they think of themselves as autonomous precisely because of neoliberal government neglect—where they become the "sphere of society that organizes itself in an autonomous way in opposition to the sphere that has been established by the State" (Esteva 2001, 13).

The role of coloniality of power creates visible tension between the political white elite and the communities and social/ethnic groups who would not conform to the cultural hegemony (Quijano, 1998). Martinez Luna (2015) argues that the world is "awakening from the illusion of a universal culture shaped by one hegemonic form of reasoning." Drawing from Oaxacan thought he uses the concept of *comunalidad* (communalism) to discuss how social actors confront "the individualism imposed as part of the logic of colonialism, privatization, and mercantilism, which are developed according to a philosophy centered in the individual as the axis of the universe." Indeed, Stahler-Sholk (2017) shows that the emphasis on autonomy in social movements in Latin America "demonstrates how people are mobilizing to govern themselves and reconfigure their political and social lives around notions of community" (13). While comunalidad is rooted in Oaxacan thought and experience, the four elements that define it—territory, governance, labor, and enjoyment—help us understand the social practices that shape autonomy in other places. The Zapatistas, according to Martinez Luna, "pulled away the blanket under which we were hidden. Now here we are, reclaiming our comunalidad."[2]

In order to best understand the ways in which the women of Maclovio Rojas practice and define autonomy in their own lives, I'd like to compare it to the struggle of the Zapatistas in Chiapas. In fact, the leadership of Maclovio Rojas has recognized their own struggles for land as being similar to those of the Zapatistas. As the Maclovio Rojas newsletter, *El Boletin Zapata* (June 2002), explained in an editorial, "This is the community that in the moments of greatest danger lifted the flag of Zapata and built the first and only *Aguascalientes* in Baja California, challenging the political and military repression of the Mexican nation-state." Hortensia described their decision of building the two-story Aguascalientes in response to the international call made by the Zapatistas in 1996:

> Nuestra lucha es la misma . . . se nos niega viviendas, escuelas, y cuidados médicos, así que lo construimos nosotros mismos . . . cuando la llamada se hizo por [el Subcomandante] Marcos [para crear el Aguascalientes] colectivamente decidimos construirlo e invitamos a muchas organizaciones nacionales e internacionales para enseñarles que esto iba a ser un lugar en donde todas estas organizaciones se pueden reunir, que este espacio era para todos.

(Our struggle is the same . . . we are denied housing, schools, and health care, so we build them on our own . . . when the call was made by [Subcomandante] Marcos [to create the Aguascalientes] we decided collectively to build it and we invited many national and international organizations to show that this was going to be a place for all of these organizations to meet, that the space was for everybody.)

In 1997, an image of Hortensia Hernández appeared on the front page of the *Wall Street Journal's* California section, with a caption referring to her as "Sub-Comandante Hortensia." The reference to the EZLN made Hyundai corporate officers and San Diego's Republican mayor, Susan Golding, quite nervous. The article, although important for getting the attention of corporate investors by pointing out strong U.S. support, misleads the reader by making a reference to Hernández as being part of the political arm of the EZLN. The week after the article was published, Hortensia Hernández, the poblado's committee, and Hyundai's officers issued a correction in a press conference conducted in the poblado: that the residents of Maclovio Rojas support and identify with the struggle being waged by the EZLN and the Indigenous communities in Chiapas. The poblado's organization, however, did not represent the political arm of the Zapatistas—in fact there was no official "political arm" of the EZLN (Mancillas, 2001).

However, aligning themselves with the Zapatistas gave Maclovianos the language to define their experience. For example, early in their struggle the Indigenous Zapatistas declared autonomous zones in their territories, but did not seek to declare political sovereignty to create their own nation-state or to pursue independence from the Mexican nation-state (Diaz-Polanco 1997). Their concern lies in pursuing guarantees in exercising their rights rather than separating from the State (Stavenhagen 1999). In other words, the Zapatistas have articulated an ideology in which "un mundo donde quepan muchos mundos" (a world in which many worlds exist), demonstrating that there is not a single Indigenous community, but, in fact, multiple voices that create multiple definitions of autonomy (Mattiace 2002). The Zapatistas do not ask for integration, but to determine the terms of engagement.

This particular claim for Indigenous autonomy in Mexico has informed the ways in which "urban marginals" (Esteva and Prakash 1999) have also articulated autonomy as a new political demand, resulting in local autonomy, which can take different shapes. In Maclovio Rojas, a rights-based framework has shaped the community's evolution into an autonomous movement; Maclovianas/os do not seek separation from the State, but they do demand full recognition as citizens with rights to land.[3] Some may argue that this serves the neoliberal project as individualist, or, worse, self-serving (Dolhinow, 2006). Instead I build on Devon Peña's (2005) idea that "autonomy is grounded in the actual struggles, discursive practices and knowledge systems of grassroots communities of resistance" (137), which in this case make a collective claim to land rights akin to those that preceded changes to Article 27 of the 1917 Mexican Constitution.

Moreover, Maclovianas seek to retain control of their settlement, and they express this through an engagement with community-centered projects. Essentially, through this practice, the women have started to develop their leadership and deepen their understanding of their lived practice of autonomy; just as Blackwell (2004) argues that the Zapatista women were able to expand the struggle for autonomy to include autonomy of the body, Maclovianas have articulated three concepts that help define the practice in their community both politically and conceptually: *necesidad* (necessity), community citizenship (defined as the interrelationship between identifying as Maclovianas and Mexicanas), and unity as a praxis of solidarity and resilience. In the following three sections, I expand on each of these articulations.

Necesidad and the Practice of Autonomy

When the leadership of Maclovio Rojas declared their settlement an autonomous one, they did so in response to the denial of basic human services both by federal and state governments—in other words, in the space of neoliberal neglect. Organizing for basic services, education for their children, and health care was driven by necessity, rather than an ideological or explicitly political conviction. In his work on *colonos* [residents] in Mexico City, Diaz-Barriga (1998) argues that the concept of necesidad is at the center of the political culture of urban grassroots organizing. Colonos include necesidad as part of their understanding of poverty, grassroots mobilization, and political co-optation, making it a source of creative tension and political mobilization. For the women of Maclovio Rojas, necesidad is the source of creative tension that first draws them to the community as a response to the structural violence they have lived, and, once they are settled, through an emerging political consciousness that compels them to act against the patriarchal social relations at home and in their engagement with the State and its enactment of neoliberal policies. For women migrants who settle along the border, the need to plant roots obligates them to act despite the obstacles that may emerge with a land takeover. Elizabeth's and Luz's narratives below exemplify this priority:

El primer año fue muy, muy duro. En realidad no teníamos nada, pero lo que teníamos lo trajimos aquí cargando en nuestras espaldas. En cuanto llegamos, pues, no teníamos casa así que del columpio de mi hija hicimos un techecito para poner la cama de mi hija y allí es donde dormían mis hijas y nosotros nos dormíamos afuera en el suelo al aire libre. Fue difícil. Pero, cuando llegamos, una de mis hijas, que entonces tenía cinco o seís, suspiró y dijo: "Por fin tengo un pedacito de tierra en donde vivir." (Elizabeth)

(That first year was very, very hard. We didn't have anything really, but anything we did have we brought here carrying it on our backs. Once we arrived, well, we didn't have a house so from my daughter's swing we made a little roof to put my daughter's bed in and that's where my daughters slept and we slept outside on the ground in the open air. It was difficult. But, when we arrived one of my daughters, who was five or six at the time, sighed and said: "Finally I have a little plot of land to live on.") (Elizabeth)

En aquel entonces el zacate llegaba arriba de tu cabeza, y mi esposo traía las vacas para acá para comer y las llevaba al acueducto para tomar agua así que decía que toda esta área estaba vacía, vacía, vacía. Cuando nos asignaron un terreno, mi esposo nos tapaba con una cobija para que no nos mojáramos y nos dormíamos sobre cartón. Allí es donde dormía a mis hijas, también. Cocinaba sobre el fuego hasta que Dios nos dio para hacernos una casa, estaba chiquita pero nos protegía del frío y el agua. Así vivimos por tres años, y los problemas solo venían cuando llovía, y mi esposo trataba de taparnos y colgar algo, pero cuando los niños estaban enfermos y mojados era muy duro . . . pero gracias a Dios seguimos adelante. (Luz)

(Back then the grass was above your head, and my husband would bring the cows this way to eat and would take them to the aqueduct to drink water, so he says that this whole area was empty, empty, empty. When we were assigned a plot of land, my husband covered us with a blanket so we wouldn't get wet and we slept on cardboard. That's where I put my daughters to sleep, too. I cooked on the fire until God gave us [the resources] to make a house, it was tiny but it protected us from the cold and water. So we lived like that for three years, and the problems only came when it rained, and my husband would try to give us shelter and put something up, but when the kids were sick and wet it was so hard . . . but thanks to God we keep moving forward.) (Luz)

Both women describe the unused lands on which they first squatted and the hardships that come with that experience, both for themselves and their children. In fact, as early residents, they had to fend off wild animals, including rattlesnakes, in the night to protect their families. But, all the while, necesidad drove them to push forward and create a collective resilience that led to political awakening. Elizabeth elaborated:

Por la necesidad que tenemos por un lugar para vivir, para poder dejarles algo a nuestros hijos, algo para el futuro. Así me siento. Tenemos la necesidad de un lugar para vivir, por eso nos hemos quedado por tanto tiempo, porque lo necesitamos.

(Because of the need that we have for somewhere to live, to be able to leave something to our children, something for the future. That's how I feel. We are in need of a place to live, that's why we have stayed so long, because we need it.)

Here the concept of necesidad is not just about meeting basic needs like housing, food, water, health care, and education—all of which are systematically denied by the political economy of neoliberal neglect. Instead, this gets translated into a political project, emerging from a women-centered political subjectivity. Hortensia explained:

La necesidad ha hecho a nuestra comunidad autónoma . . . si tienes a un niño que va creciendo y buscas a las escuelas en las comunidades alrededor, ellos no te van a dejar poner a tu hijo en sus escuelas porque según ellos eres un invasor, un delincuente. Si buscas trabajo en una maquiladora y se dan cuenta que vives en Maclovio Rojas, ellos no te quieren allí porque creen que eres un delincuente. Así que no tienes derecho a seguro social si a tus papás no les dan trabajo. Hasta la policía no nos cuida, nos reprimen. Si el gobierno no nos da lo que necesitamos, nos obligan a organizarnos sólos. Así que construímos nuestras escuelas, creamos un campo de deporte, y lo hicimos todo trabajando juntos. Por eso somos autónomos, no nos han dado absolutamente nada más que problemas.

(Necessity has made the community autonomous . . . if you have a growing child and you seek out the schools in the neighboring communities, they will not let you put your child in their schools because in their eyes you are an invader, a delinquent. If you look for work in a maquiladora and they find out you live in Maclovio Rojas, they don't want you there because they think you are a delinquent. So, you don't have a right to social security if your parents aren't given work. Even the police don't take care of us, they repress us. If the government doesn't give us what we need, then they obligate us to organize ourselves. So we built our schools, we created a sports field, and we did it all working together. This is why we are autonomous, we haven't been given absolutely anything [by the State] but problems.)

These narratives reveal several qualities about this form of autonomous resistance and self-organizing. First, they show that meeting basic necessities becomes a vehicle for organizing the community on a political level, as well as to meet the needs left unmet as a consequence of neoliberal neglect. Second, these narratives underscore a Mexican working-class mistrust of police authority, especially given the history of the use of police, military force, and for-hire thugs to violently suppress workers and community movements. Third, they demonstrate how the source of tensions with the neoliberal State derive from women's desire to provide not only a foundation but a future for their children and their community. Maclovianas were not seeking an alternative way of life; they simply wanted what has been denied to them. Their solution? Doing it themselves. The successful completion of multiple projects materializes their quest for autonomy: as examples of spaces of survival and sociopolitical action in which they are building noncapitalist social relations (Zibechi 2012).

Hortensia explained:

Con tiempo Maclovio Rojas ha crecido, y, como comunidad, decidimos que no nos podíamos esperar hasta que nos entregaran "oficialmente" las tierras porque los niños creciendo en la comunidad necesitaban escuela, los adultos necesitaban un espacio para su crecimiento personal. Nuestro primer objetivo fue la tierra, para cosecharla, para criar animales, y como eso no pasó, y teníamos la tierra, tuvimos que hacer algo. Decidimos distribuir las tierras y crear una infraestructura económica, cultural y educativa. De allí salieron las ideas para todos nuestros proyectos, y en 1992 construimos nuestra primera escuela de primaria porque no podíamos dejar que nuestros hijos estuvieran sin escuela. En todos estos años hemos buscado maneras de crear mejores modos de vivir para los residentes de Maclovio Rojas y si tenemos este espacio, tenemos que ver cómo lo vamos a dividir para buscar un futuro digno para todos en cada manera.

(With time Maclovio Rojas has grown, and, as a community, we decided that we couldn't wait until the lands were "officially" granted to us because the kids growing in the community need schooling, the adults need space for personal growth. Our first objective was the land, to harvest it, to raise animals, and since that didn't happen, and we had the land, we had to do something. We decided to distribute the lands and create an economic, cultural, and educational infrastructure. This is where the ideas for all of our projects emerged, and in 1992 we built our first elementary school because we couldn't let the kids be without schooling. In all of these years we have looked for ways to create better living situations for the residents of Maclovio Rojas and if we have this space, we need to see how we are going to divide it to look for a dignified future for everyone in all ways.)

As Dora elaborated:

> El gobierno no ha invertido ni un centavo en nuestra comunidad, pero a pesar de eso, la comunidad ha hecho dos primarias, una secundaria, una guardería, un centro de mujeres, un centro comunitario/salones de reunión, un cementerio, el tianguis, queremos construir una universidad en el cerro/cima para estudiar filosofía/estudios políticos. También queremos construir una escuela para adultos y una casa de ancianos.

> (The government hasn't invested one dime in our community, but despite this, the community has made two elementary schools, a middle school, a child care center, a women's center, a community center/meeting rooms, a cemetery, the swap meet; we want to build a university on the plateau/hill to study philosophy/political studies. We also want to build an adult school and a retirement home.)

Necesidad has driven Maclovianas to reconceptualize their lives as mothers and community members and to provide for their families in ways that they themselves could not imagine before arriving. In so doing they adopt organizational forms that perhaps start from the family, but are also from units that are not nuclear families, ending up forming stable and extended relationships of support (Zibechi 2012). Sylvia explained to me:

> uno viene aquí necesitando tierra pero cuando estas aquí empiezas a ver . . . es como cuando entra a una cocina y quizás tienes una idea de lo que vas a cocinar, pero en cuanto empiezas, ves algo más, y ves otra idea de lo que vas a hacer. Antes no tenía tantas ideas, y ahora que he estado aquí, me he despertado. Si nunca has batallado de esta manera o has vivido de esta manera, te encuentras con algo nuevo, pero viene de la necesidad de uno que te da la fuerza para enfrentar lo que se te presenta. Eso es lo que me ha mantenido aquí.

(one comes here needing land but once you're here you start seeing . . . it's like when you enter a kitchen and maybe you have an idea about what you're going to cook, but once you start, you see something else, and you see another idea about what you want to make. I didn't use to have so many ideas, and now that I've been here, I've woken up. If you've never struggled in this way or lived in this way, then you are confronted with something new, but it stems from one's need which makes one strong to face whatever may come. This is what has kept me here.)

By fulfilling their basic needs, women are creating alternative experiences and possibilities, with a woman-centered vision that differs from other poblados. While women are at the forefront of most UPMs in Mexico, their "activist" mothering operates vis-à-vis the State; in Maclovio Rojas they no longer take their demands to the State and instead take stock of their needs and act collectively. The day care center at the Casa de la Mujer had been in operation for about a month when I first arrived, and within several weeks approximately fifteen children were in attendance. Parents, primarily single-moms, take advantage of the (U.S.) ten-dollar-a-week childcare—an essentially symbolic fee, since it does not even cover the cost of even the food that the children are provided. It is important to make childcare accessible, though, since the mothers work primarily at the maquiladoras, and their own salary would not make any other option feasible. Herein, of course, lies a major contradiction. The majority of the women do have to depend on the multinational companies for employment, for a waged labor. For this too, however, they blame the State—for not allowing their community projects to grow, including the family farmland they had hoped would sustain their community. Instead, they are forced to fight legal battles, defend their land, and organize in order to maintain their residencies and, if successful, the right to food sovereignty or to grow their own crops.

What remains true is that their commitment is shaped by an idea of woman-centered communal autonomy. Through these material tactics, Maclovianas legitimize women's needs and build alternatives, both conceptually and politically—conceptually because, through their lived practice of autonomy, shaped by their necesidad, Maclovianas develop a definition of their experience. Paula summarized it well:

> Para ser libre y soberano, para que sea absoluto, que esto sea sólo Maclovio Rojas y nadie más, que el gobierno no venga y nos diga que hacer, queremos poder decidir como Maclovianas lo que queremos. Si queremos algo verde, pues, y luego, tiene que ser verde porque así lo queremos. Que estemos absolutamente solos, si hay una Casa de la Mujer o un centro de guardería, es porque lo hemos hecho. Si estamos conectados a agua, es porque lo hemos amañado; todos trabajando juntos lo ha hecho posible. Si hay una primaria o secundaria, es porque nosotros mismos nos pusimos de frente para que se hiciera y porque hemos presionado a las autoridades que nos dieran la clave. Por eso tenemos escuelas. Hemos trabajado largo y duro para tener lo que tenemos. El Centro de Estudios Filosóficos es algo que hemos hecho juntos, aplanamos el cerro para que algún día la escuela se construye. Con esta escuela los estudiantes pueden seguir sus estudios después de la preparatoria. Las calles, todos hemos trabajado juntos para abrir los pasajes para las calles para poder ir y venir cuando queramos para que las calles sean mejor, especialmente cuando se llenan de lodo en temporada de lluvias. Nosotros, como comunidad, hemos estado presentes hemos juntado dinero, hecho bailes, fiestas, hemos hecho muchas cosas para poder tener lo que tenemos.

> (To be free and sovereign, that it be absolute, that this only be Maclovio Rojas and nobody else, that the government doesn't come in and tell us what to do, we want to be able to decide as Maclovianas what we want. If we want something green, well, then, it needs to be green because

that's what we want. That we are absolutely on our own, if there's a Casa de la Mujer or a childcare center, it's because we have done it. If we are connected to water, it's because we have rigged it; everyone working together has made it happen. If there's an elementary or middle school, it's because we have put ourselves out there to try and make it happen and because we have pressured the authorities to give us the clave.[4] That's why we have the schools. We have worked long and hard to have what we have. The Centro de Estudios Filosóficos [the site for the future university] is something that we have done together, we flattened the hillside so that at one point the school could be built. With this school the students can continue their studies beyond high school. The streets, we have all worked together to open the passageways for the streets to be able to come and go as we please, so that the streets can be better, especially when they get covered in mud during the rainy season. We as a community have been present, we have had fundraisers, organized dances, parties, we have done many things to be able to have what we have.)

In vividly recapturing the driving force of the residents—the failure of the State to meet their needs—Paula frames the political project of their woman-centered vision as one that creates possibilities and education for all. It moves beyond necesidad and marks a kind of transnational feminist progress that transcends basic needs and basic rights.[5] Through their collective efforts, Maclovianas take ownership of their community and redefine the possibilities of their lives.

Teresa agreed:

Hemos trabajado duro, por ejemplo, la Casa de la Mujer en donde el centro de guardería está, nosotras fuimos las que la iniciamos, nosotras la apoyamos en varias maneras, unas trabajaron, otras donaron dinero y, pues, ahora está allí. El cementerio, lo encercamos, la escuela, Niños de Baja California, nosotros en la comunidad lo hicimos posible. Mis hijos no asistieron a la escuela pero mis nietos benefician de ella. Con todos los proyectos todo hemos cooperado con el material, con trabajar o donar dinero . . . ves, las tierras no solo nos las dieron, nos las merecemos por todo nuestro esfuerzo.

(We have worked hard, for example, the Casa de la Mujer where the childcare center is, we were the ones to initiate it, we supported it in various ways, some would work, others would donate money and, well, now it's there. The cemetery, we fenced it off, the school, Niños de Baja California, we in the community made it happen. My children didn't attend the school but my grandchildren are benefiting from it. With all of the projects we have all cooperated either with [building] materials, by working or by donating money . . . you see, the lands haven't just been given to us, we've earned them through a lot of our effort.)

And it is that effort that distinguishes Maclovianas from the government and its elected officials. Dora asserted:

El gobierno presiona mucho a los líderes de movimientos sociales porque el compromiso que tienen con la gente es puro, no corrupto o sucio como el del gobierno, sólo piensan en dinero. Por ejemplo, en realidad soy vendedora, pero lo renuncié todo sin esperar nada de regreso. Pero estoy satisfecha porque salgo a la calle y quizás una mujer se me acerque y me saluda y me ofrece un pedazo de chicle o un vaso de agua. Así que, me pregunto, ¿pórque hace eso? Es porque he dado algo de mí aquí, ayudo a la gente. Es algo grande.

(The government puts a lot of pressure on all leaders of social movements because their commitment to the people is pure, not corrupted and dirty like the government's, they only think of money. For example, I'm really a vendor, but I gave it all up without expecting anything in return. But I'm satisfied because I go out to the street and maybe a woman will approach me to say hi and offer me a piece of gum or

a glass of water. So, I ask myself, why does she do that? It's because
I have given something of myself here, I help people. It's something
big.)

Necesidad, as the source of creative tension, guided the women
and their families to build a community on the lands in order to build
homes for their families. In witnessing the inaction of the state and
federal government, Maclovianas came together to develop their
community and have come to place value in their efforts, hard work,
and dedication, using this as a platform to further articulate their
rights to their land and their right to determine their community's
fate. Moreover, they share a vision that the nation-state cannot envision. This, in fact, can obstruct the effects of structural violence. Here
again the work of the Maclovianas asks us to consider the concept
of the *commons*: the poblado as a site that has recuperated collective
lands but also, as Gonzalez (2011) argues, as an example of social
movement that is working *through* commons, toward mutuality
through horizontal social networks.

Community Citizenship: *Porque Somos Mexicanos*

Gender is an essential element in the construction of nations (Craske
2005). Gendered nationalism scripts for women (and men) a particular
role to play—as women in the political sphere (as seen in women's citizenship), in the cultural sphere (as representatives of national honor
or symbolic of the nation itself), or in the socioeconomic sphere (as
reproducers of workers, as wageworkers and consumers). During the
nation-building project following the Mexican Revolution, "women's
inclusion in the new, modern Mexico was represented more clearly in
cultural and socio-economic terms than in the political arena" (118).
Though Mexico granted rights to women in the socioeconomic sphere,

as enshrined in the Mexican Constitution of 1917, women's traditional socioeconomic role in reproduction remained prevalent, and, with it, the reinforcing of cultural stereotypes that see women as self-sacrificing and community-oriented for the sake of the nation and not their own agency or desires. This view of women is embedded in the Mexican nation's auto-referential narrative, as well as in women's domestic roles, and purports, in particular, that women's importance comes from their influence over third persons—children, the family, and, by extension, the nation. "Women's role was acknowledged to be important for the state, but not sufficiently so for women to be given a political voice or citizenship rights" (120) in Mexico.

Culturally defined expectations of women partly explain the lack of investment in their education and preparation for participation in the socioeconomic and political spheres. Instead, culturally defined expectations of women offer another right-turned-privilege: the right to be poor as the right to state-sanctioned premature death (Gilmore 2007). To illustrate this point on a national level, in 2000, 11.7 percent of women age fifteen and older had no education, a little more than 50 percent had some schooling, and only 9.4 percent had managed to attain higher education. Mexico's own lack of investment in women has set the stage for both local and multinational companies to open their doors, offering ten- to twelve-hour shifts in domestic service, restaurants, and small factories without any guarantees or benefits, and often in temporary, informal work (INEGI 2005; Olivera 2010). The consequence of this disproportionate violence against certain bodies is the continued feminization of poverty and the exploitation of women without consequence or accountability.

The dualistic nature of women's citizenship began by excluding women from key aspects of citizenship while simultaneously giving them small gains in political space and identity. The discourse of the revolutionary family has mostly continued to be embodied by the State, although the student movements of 1968 did provide an opportunity for young women to step into a world of public action that erased traditional boundaries between public and private and moved them toward a political participation that challenged authoritarian structures on many levels (Cohen and Frazier 2009; Evans 2009). By the time Carlos Salinas de Gortari became president in 1988, women were, legally, equal citizens with men, although access to that citizenship was constrained by socioeconomic expectations that placed women at a disadvantage in practical terms (Craske 2005).

Citizenship is a contested practice that operates as a mechanism for both inclusion and exclusion; for Mexican women, exclusion has been institutionalized and codified into law and practice. But, as Lister (2003) argues, citizenship is also pivotal to the definition and interpretation of needs and to the struggle for their realization and conversion into rights. Holston (2008) makes a similar argument based on his ethnographic work in Brazil when he uses the concept of insurgent citizenship to demonstrate how citizens confront inequities with alternative formulations of citizenship to access rights. In Maclovio Rojas, the women invoke their citizenship and their right to land "porque somos mexicanos" [because we are Mexicans]. Yet expressions of citizenship and national identity are appealed to by the very families who are waging a contentious battle for land with/against the State. They come to identify national citizenship in terms of a "rights framework," but, in terms of belonging and communal identity, their affinity is to Maclovio Rojas. In order to exist and to move forward, they must be able to depend on one another, giving rise to the collective sense of belonging as Macloviano/as. To illustrate this point, Juana stated, "Estamos enseñando al gobierno que no es necesario que estén presente para que nuestra comunidad progrese" (We are showing the government that it's not necessary for them to be present in order for a community to get ahead).

Paula added:

Hemos tenido problemas porque el gobierno quiere entrar y los líderes no los quiere, y, pues, allí estamos. Me gusta aquí, pues, porque valoramos lo que temenos. Sabemos el sacrificio que se necesita para construir lo poquito que tenemos, el trabajo que se requiere para escarbar una zanja, hasta para comprar clavos, hay mucho sacrificio aquí y lo valoramos mucho.

(We have had problems because the government wants to come in and the leaders don't want them to, and, well, that's where we're at. I like it here, though, because we value what we have. We know the sacrifice it takes to build up the little that we have, the labor it requires to make a ditch, to buy nails, even, there is a lot of sacrifice here, and we value it a lot.)

This is a sentiment that holds true for most women I spoke with; there is a value in the work they have done, in the sacrifice, both personally and collectively, it has taken to create what they have. Their affinity to Maclovio Rojas and the recognition of their efforts allows them to critique the State. I'm reminded again of the sign at the entrance to the Aguascalientes that remains true thirty years later: "El lema del gobierno es dividir y conquistar y la de Maclovio es: la unión hace la fuerza porque lo hemos demostrado con más de 15 años de lucha" (The motto of the government is divide and conquer and Maclovio's is: there is strength in unity because we have demonstrated it with over fifteen years of struggle).

Through their perseverance, the Maclovianas articulate a critique of the neoliberal state. They reveal and ridicule its corruption and its destructive and repressive policies. Beyond this critique they have also articulated a "rights"-based framework for a movement mobilization that is not a Trojan horse of neoliberal "individual" rights (Esteva and Prakash 1999). Instead, the Maclovianas embrace a rights narrative that values unity, struggle, and sacrifice for the right to establish and sustain livelihoods and secure, stable communities through collective action and comunalidad. This has allowed them to develop a woman-centered political subjectivity to move their own development projects forward. Essentially, they use a variant of "nationalist" discourse—in this case, asserting the common bonds of Mexicanidad—to insert themselves into the political process. By doing so, however, they subvert hegemonic definitions of national identity because, as the racialized, working-class, female poor—*el Mexico profundo*—they were never truly meant to form part of that "nation-building" civic discourse.

Given that their loyalty remains grounded in the struggle to fulfill the needs of the community itself, they evade the individualizing logics of neoliberalism and operate within a framework that embodies what I call *community citizenship*. As Dora described it:

> Los niños también son Mexicanos, así que tienen derecho a una educación, no como los hijos de los oficiales del gobierno que mandan a sus hijos a escuelas privadas. El dinero que usan para pagar la colegiatura es de nuestros impuestos mientras, aquí, nuestros hijos los abandonan.

> (The kids here are also Mexicanos, so they have a right to an education, not like the children of the government officials who send their children to private schools. The money they use to pay for their fees is our tax money while, here, our children are abandoned.)

Moreover, when Elizabeth made the decision to stay she made it because she knew the lands were national territory, not privately owned, and she, like any other citizen, had a right to stay.

There is a maternal dimension to this sense of the Macloviana assertion of community citizenship. The obligations to care for children are not framed in terms of captivity to patriarchal or neoliberal norms. Once again, there is a commitment to a collective intergenerational sense of justice. Elizabeth argued that the residents have a right to stay because of their labor and struggle:

De todo el sufrimiento que hemos soportado, por muchos años no teníamos agua o electricidad, nada. Antes comprabamos grandes tambos de agua, y nos cobraban mucho, y usabamos velas y gas por luz. Estuvimos así por muchos años. Por eso te digo, hemos sufrido mucho, todos nosotros y por eso siento que tenemos el derecho, bien ganado, para vivir aquí.

(Of all of the suffering we have endured, for many years we didn't have water or electricity, nothing. We used to buy big containers of water, and they charged us a lot, and we used candles and gas for light. We were like that for many years. That's why I tell you, we have suffered a lot, all of us and that's why I feel we have the right, rightly won, to live here.)

Their resolve to stay and their inherent understanding of their rights as Mexican citizens parallels the Zapatista invocation of nationalism "nunca más un México sin nosotros" (never again a Mexico without us). The call of the Zapatistas for a new world stirred up intense political debates because they were not only calling for change; they were seeking recognition as citizens, as Mexicanos.

Desde el principio de nuestro levantamiento, y antes, los Zapatistas Indígenas siempre han insistido que somos Mexicanos pero también Indígenas. Eso quiere decir que demandemos un lugar en la nación Mexicana pero sin dejar atrás quienes somos. De esta entrada histórica va emerger no sólo un México mejor y justo, pero un nuevo México también. En esto apostamos nuestras vidas, para que la próxima generación de Mexicanos tengan un país en donde no es desgracia vivir. México le pertenece a los Mexicanos. Que se levante todo México. Tierras Mexicanas. La gente indígena es Mexicana, una llamada nacional para la unidad.

(From the beginning of our uprising, and before, the Indigenous Zapatistas have always insisted that we are Mexicans but also Indigenous. That means we demand a place in the Mexican nation but without leaving behind who we are. From this historic entryway will emerge not only a better and more just Mexico, but a new Mexico as well. On this we bet our lives, so that the next generation of Mexicans will have a country in which it is not a disgrace to live. Mexico belongs to the Mexicans. Rise up all of Mexico. Mexican lands. Indigenous peoples are Mexicans, a national call for unity.) (EZLN 1995)

In both the narratives of the Maclovianas and the Zapatista declarations exists a commitment to the next generations. This is underscored by the women-centered political subjectivity explored in the previous chapter.

The Zapatistas' promotion of their cause as nationalist, while also promoting "diversality" (Grosfoguel 2002; Mignolo 2000), has challenged static definitions of social movements, particularly in Mexico. Being able to name the local experience as an important and valid political reference, while creating links with the nation-state at large, fundamentally challenges the classic dichotomy of political change that imposes a top-down, state-directed process of adaptation and co-optation of local constituencies. The Zapatistas have sought autonomy from the State, but not separation. They have declared the State to be illegitimate and, consequently, direct no demands toward it. Instead, they direct their autonomy toward the process of new, collectively enacted social and political formations by creating awareness around the multiple possibilities for change, which has led the movement to fashion a process of Indigenous-led ideological transformation—apart from the interpellation of the neoliberal state—and thus foment a space for autonomy. This combination of actions has made Zapatismo the principal social force to drive the "legitimation crisis" within the neoliberal Mexican state while transforming local communities so they can join in the ever-multiplying place-based experiments in local self-determination and autonomy. As Forbis (2015) argues, the Zapatistas both affirm and deny Mexican identity where they expose the complexities, the contradictions and paradoxes, underlying the new geographies of belonging constructed by them. The Zapatistas' "collectivity has derived from nonliberal nationalism a call for bottom-up democracy—not where the multitude fits into one world, but for *un mundo donde quepan muchos mundos* (a world where many worlds fit). By tying their vision of Mexico to radical democracy, the Zapatistas challenge the assertion that any nationalism not based solely on liberal notions of individual rights is inherently anti-democratic and oppressive" (378).

Like the Zapatistas, the Maclovianas/os are not trying to take over the state, even if they already know that they, the people, actually *are* the "nation"—the multiple subjectivities comprising the "constituent power" (Hardt and Negri 2011). They demand recognition but not "integration" into the neoliberal political project, which they reject. Their demands for recognition of themselves in their difference—*somos iguales porque somos diferentes*—are really about securing the rights to the land they have developed; yet still they claim their status as free and independent producers and community. Maria explained:

> Tenemos que seguir progresando como gente y como comunidad, tenemos los mismos derechos que una comunidad rica. Tenemos el derechos de vivir como queremos vivir, tenemos el derecho de vivir decentemente y no nos podemos esperar a que ellos nos lo traigan, tenemos que luchar por él. Después de 16 años en Maclovio Rojas, la comunidad se ha acostumbrado a buscar lo que necesita y no esperar que el gobierno va a cumplir . . . así que tenemos que seguir planeando y trabajando juntos para conseguir lo que necesitamos igual como los demás Mexicanos todos los demás seres humanos. *No nos podemos quedar aquí aislados esperando que el gobierno nos tire migajas.*

(We have to keep progressing as people and as community, we have the same rights as a rich community does. We have the right to live how we want to live, we have the right to live decently and we can't wait for them to bring it to us we have to fight for it. After sixteen years in Maclovio Rojas, the community has become accustomed to seeking out what it needs and not waiting for the government to follow through . . . so we have to continue planning and working together to get what we need just like all Mexicans or all human beings. *We can't be here isolated waiting for the government to throw us the crumbs.*) (emphasis added)

While critical of the neoliberal state, these narratives demonstrate how women identify themselves as part of a national identity, giving them the right to fight for the lands they sit on, even if it means fighting against the state and federal government. As Dora says, "We are not animals, we are mexicanos." They demand to be recognized as citizens on their own terms.

Even though women have been erased historically in the Mexican national imagination, Maclovianas clearly feel very connected to the nation. As Sassen (2003) argues, "Citizenship is partly produced by the practices of the excluded" (22), which creates new discourse around loyalty and allegiance producing what she calls "effective nationality and informal citizenship" (2005, 85) The full citizens who are not recognized as political subjects, such as housewives and mothers, are precisely the ones who engender this new discourse. Maclovianas disrupt nationalist discourse about citizenship by appropriating that which they deem beneficial, such as rights to land because they are Mexican citizens, while simultaneously critiquing the neoliberal nation-state and its ties to capital and transnational companies. Their location, now almost entirely engulfed by industrial parks, and its proximity to the U.S.-Mexico border, vividly reveals the contradictions of global capital and state neglect. Through their commitment to their community, Maclovianas exemplify community citizenship as a form of belonging that appeals to "effective nationality" without being beholden to formal state policies.

Sassen (2005) contends that the urban space of the global city is especially salient for the repositioning of citizenship in practice— dynamics that signal the possibilities for a membership simultaneously localized and transnational. As Lister (2003) highlights, women's participation in informal politics should be recognized as a legitimate form of political citizenship. For the women of Maclovio Rojas, their activism constructs their political citizenship; they invoke their rights as Mexicanas while maintaining an allegiance to Maclovio Rojas. They draw from both of these experiences to make claims to their rights: rights to land, to state representation, and to self-determine their community as residents. As Maclovianas have articulated it, through their own sweat, blood, and tears they have earned the right to be recognized as local citizens of the community and, in turn, the right of the community to exist.

For example, in Maclovio Rojas, the struggle for land is, of course, at the base of the movement, but the struggle for the basic services of water and power also complicate the daily living conditions for the Maclovianas/os. If the community is "regularized" and recognized as a "legal" entity with the residents gaining the land titles, the state and municipal government would bring in the infrastructure for the basic services. Dora addressed the centrality of water in particular:

> Tenemos que robar agua y luz porque el gobierno no quiere darnos estos servicios, tenemos un sin fin de pedidos documentados. El agua no esta procesada, está sucia pero igual la usamos y ahora estamos pagando por ella con la encarcelación de nuestra compañera. No somos los únicos que nos robamos el agua. La academia policiaca también se roba el agua y dos maquilas, y los establos allí en frente pero a ellos no los están demandando, sólo a nosotros.

(We have to steal water and power because the government doesn't want to provide us with the services, we have an infinite number of requests documented. The water is not processed, it's dirty water and we use it anyway and now we're paying for it with the incarceration of our *compañera*. We are not the only ones who steal the water. The police academy also steals the water and two maquilas, and the stables in front but they aren't suing them, only us.)

The contradictions are blatant. Yet Maclovio Rojas does not seek power and does not aim to create its own government; in fact, the leaders and residents are willing to be regularized as long as the government respects their projects. This they are adamant about. Dora insisted:

No estamos pidiendo regularización, si va ser regularizado pues, está bien, pero debe de incluir nuestras bases comunitarias. El gobierno puede entrar, pero no vamos a pagar por las tierras otra vez, porque estas tierras ya están pagadas. Se pagaron en el 1994. Nuestra meta es seguir luchando, salir adelante, que continuemos siendo una comunidad autónoma. Vamos a ofrecerle al gobierno las siguientes condiciones: no reducen las tierras, respeten las tierras entregadas, y no quitar nuestros proyectos. No queremos que el gobierno llegue a tomar control y que se beneficie de nuestros sacrificios porque aquí para donar digamos un ladrillo, la gente ha tenido que trabajar duro. Esto pertenece a la comunidad.

(We're not asking for regularization, if it's going to be regularized well, then good, but it will have to include our community bases. The government can come in, but we're not going to pay for the lands again, because these lands have already been paid. They were paid in 1994. Our goal is to keep fighting, to move forward that we continue to be an autonomous community. We will offer the government the following conditions: no reduction of the lands, respect the given lands, and not to remove our projects. We don't want the government to take over and benefit from our sacrifices, because here, in order to donate let's say a brick, the people have had to work a lot. This belongs to the community.)

Maclovianas/os both reject and use the State to move their project forward. Residents want their lands to become regularized (i.e., recognized by the State), yet they want to retain control of the structure of the community and their projects and continue to have a voice in the future of their land settlement. They will not relinquish all they have gained, both materially and ideologically. The majority of residents may not be able to name Marxism, feminist theory or even Zapatismo—nor do they need to—but they know what they need and who is denying them these services: the State and its neoliberal practices. For the women of Maclovio Rojas, understanding their role in the political world then becomes a possibility. Maclovianas redefine their practice of community citizenship to the local experience vis-à-vis the State, reposition themselves as political citizens, and employ a politics of unity and solidarity.

Unity and Solidarity

Maclovianas demonstrate an allegiance to their community and to each other. As Teresa says, "Todos somos ramas del mismo árbol aquí" (We are all branches of the same tree here). Unity is a concept that has been built into the ways in which the women live their lives. As Paula reiterated, "This is not just me, it's all of us. We all have the same fears that they might drive us out or whatever, but we all have the same fear, not just me." Unity is what drives the survival of the organization, the community, and the lucha.

Sylvia talked about when she first arrived to the community:

No había tanta gente en aquel entonces, la comunidad siempre ha sido unida. Eso es algo que ha tenido Maclovio Rojas, que la gente es muy unida. Todos sabemos lo que queremos, y todos cuidamos de lo que tenemos. Yo creo que eso es lo más importante.

(There weren't a lot of people then, the community has always been united. That's something that Maclovio Rojas has had, that the people are very united. We all know what we want, and we all take care of what we have. I think that's the most important thing.)

Yet Luz cautioned that at the base of their struggle lies an ever-impending threat that must keep them focused:

Tenemos que ser unidos porque estamos en peligro de perderlo todo aunque hemos estado aquí por tantos años. Mucha gente cree que esta ya se ha ganado, pero la verdad es que todavía no, y aunque tengan sus casas construídas y han estado aquí por mucho tiempo, no quiere decir que deben de dejar de asistir a las reuniones y eso. La lucha no ha terminado. El gobierno nos tiene que dejar las 197 hectáreas que tenemos, y todavía no tenemos solución para eso. Así que tenemos que seguir nuestro trabajo. La lucha es nuestra porque, con sólo una persona no puedes hacer nada, todos tienen que ayudar.

(We have to be united because we are in danger of losing this all although we already have been here for so many years. Many people think that this has already been won, but the truth is that it hasn't, and even though they may have their homes built and have been here for a long time, it doesn't mean that they should stop attending the meetings and such. The fight is not over. The government needs to leave us the 197 hectares that we have, and we still don't have a solution to that. So we need to keep up our work. The fight is all of ours because, with one person you can't do anything, everyone has to be involved.)

Maclovianas have conceptualized their collective identity through their experience of unity and solidarity with one another. Being able to count on one another and to accompany one another has helped them get through some of their more difficult moments. Hortensia described the time she and two other leaders were incarcerated—as a result of the State Penal Code 226 discussed earlier—for being leaders of this land movement. This is when the community organized the march to the state capitol, a 135-mile walk in the middle of the desert summer months. She remembered:

> Cuando a Artemio, a Juan y a mí nos encarcelaron en agosto del 1996, ese septiembre la comunidad organizó una marcha a Mexicali. Para mí es muy bonito saber que tanta gente participó. Hasta llevaron a sus perros; unos de sus animales murieron en el camino. Unas personas aún siguen enfermos del esfuerzo, un compañero se murió de paro cardíaco, e hicieron todo eso sólo para que sus líderes sean liberados y para que el gobierno respetara sus tierras. Esta era la tercera marcha a Mexicali, habían dos antes de eso, pero este era la más difícil, y el gobierno no quería tomar la responsabilidad porque decían que los problemas eran problemas internos entre grupos y que no tenían nada que ver con eso; que en Mexicali no tenían nada que ver con el tema, que teníamos que resolver el tema en Tijuana. Así que nuestro compañero muere en el desierto acercándonos a Mexicali, si se puede imaginar el calor en el verano. Con esta desgracia nos dejaron salir [de la cárcel] en octubre.

(When Artemio,[6] Juan, and myself were jailed in August 1996, that September the community organized a march to Mexicali.[7] It's really beautiful to me to know that so many people participated. They even took their dogs, some of their animals died on the road. People are still sick to this day from the exertion, a *compañero* died from cardiac arrest, and they did all of that just so that their leaders could be freed and so that the government would respect their land. This was the third march to Mexicali, there were two before that, but this one was the hardest, and the government didn't want to take responsibility because they argued that the problems were internal problems between groups and they had nothing to do with it; that in Mexicali they had nothing to do with the issue, that we needed to handle the issue in Tijuana. So our compañero dies in the desert nearing Mexicali, if you can imagine the heat during the summer. With this disgrace we were let out [of jail] in October [1996].)

While the weight of the death of their compañero was certainly tragic and felt by all, the residents remained ever-more committed and united. In my observations, the community has survived the repressive tactics imposed by the State because they have unified against them and created their own way of life. In fact, despite the fast-paced nature of Tijuana and the looming buzz of the neighboring maquiladoras, one senses general feeling of belonging in Maclovio Rojas. As Luz describes it:

Aparte de todo, está tranquilo aquí—te puedes llevar bien con toda la gente y estás libre. No es como en la ciudad, esto es mas como un rancho en donde todos se conocen, donde todos comparten y todos quieren estar juntos. Cada año en diciembre hay posadas y eso es divertido juntarnos.

(Apart from it all, it's peaceful here—you can get along with all of the people and you're free. It's not like in the city, this is more like a ranch where everyone knows each other, where everyone shares and everyone wants to be together. Every year in December there are posadas and such, and it's fun to hang out with one another.)

The idea of collective identity is also reinforced in general meetings, assemblies and conversations with residents when the leaders remind them, "Lo que tenemos lo tenemos por nosotros" (What we have, we have because of ourselves). These sorts of comments lend importance to the collective work in the community. By reiterating their common advances, collective agency is valued and perpetuated. In creating this space, Maclovianas have developed their own definition of autonomy, one that stems from necesidad and community-centered expressions of citizenship and unifies migrants seen as disposable by the neoliberal state. This neglect inadvertently created a space for the Maclovianas to search for an autonomous path for fulfilling their collective needs. However, that pathway was not some neoliberal version of self-care and personal responsibility or the creation of the multiplex assets of the community—the school, women's center, infrastructure, and all the rest. Autonomy was not the result of privatized initiatives, but living institutions of collective action. Through their practice of unity, the Maclovianas demonstrated their resilience and asserted their emerging leadership. Women seized the gaps presented by neoliberal neglect to create a space for themselves in Maclovio Rojas to secure a future for their families. As Luz stated with conviction: "Es mi patrimonio, lo tengo que defender" (This is my patrimony, so I must defend it). To this day, Maclovio Rojas remains a community *en lucha*.

CONCLUSION

Cada uno su granito de arena

Transnational Organizing and the Future of Maclovio Rojas

I BEGAN THIS BOOK BY tracing the genealogy of neglect along the U.S.-Mexico border, a neglect grounded in a colonial relationship that has continuously subjugated and racialized Mexican women in the modern, colonial world (Hernandez 2018). Long after the end of formal colonialism, the coloniality of power continues to perpetuate differentiated forms of exploitation based on race, gender, and region (Grosfoguel 2007; Lugones 2007; Mignolo 2007; Quijano 2000). Yet the problems facing Maclovio Rojas are both old and new. The accelerated rate of globalization practices including the North American Free Trade Agreement (NAFTA) and the more recent USMCA (U.S./ Mexico/Central American Agreement) has altered conditions in northern Mexican cities, producing enormous population shifts, substandard employment in the maquiladoras, and little to no state infrastructure to ensure adequate health, housing, and educational facilities.

Neoliberal privatization policies deprive some communities of greatly needed resources, public services, and infrastructures, and women bear the burdens when the communities in which they live lack basic necessities. Systems of gendered power leave women both economically marginal and domestically central. These realities have compelled women around the world to confront their predicaments, organize in new ways, and take part in collective movements for change (Mohanty 2003; Bhavnani, Foran, and Kurian 2003). It is in these "grietas" (Zapatistas), "fissures" (Holloway 2019), or "ruptures" (Sitrin 2012) where we find openings for envisioning and creating new social and economic relationships.

Throughout this book, I have responded to my initial questions: What social realities produced opportunities for mujeres fronterizas to take matters of organization, development, and community governance into their own hands? What lessons can we derive from the narratives of their struggles for autonomy in the broadening search by social forces on both sides of the border actively seeking alternatives to neoliberal capitalism? I hope I have demonstrated how unmet need has led to unparalleled agency.

In Maclovio Rojas, women have not only worked to obtain resources and services, but they have developed a political response to neoliberal dispossession and disposability, in many ways defying the Mexican state and global capital alike by declaring their community autonomous and governing it through new collective democratic practices and institutions—reclaiming a social infrastructure at the time they reimagine community through collective forms of citizenship. They draw on their designated roles in the putatively private realms of family and child-rearing to proclaim new public identities forged through politics. The women of Maclovio Rojas struggle for autonomy—from the State, from corporations, from violent domestic partners—while simultaneously claiming their rights as citizens of the Mexican nation. As Holloway (2009) points out, movements that seek to prefigure a world that could be are "sometimes using the state but at the same time [are] against and beyond the state" (22). The tension between Maclovianas' desire for state recognition of their lands while fighting for the self-determination of their community and family is not, to them, a contradiction.

Indeed, as Dolhinow (2010) argues, "hegemonies, even the colossal neoliberal hegemony, are never complete, and it is in their gaps and openings that change and revolutions can occur" (205). Hegemonic power makes its presence relentlessly felt in Maclovio Rojas, where residents suffer from the absence of state-supported infrastructure and social services, as well as from the presence of myriad forms of structural inequality, exploitation, and violence. The influx of foreign capital, patterns of rural displacement and dispossession, and constantly shifting labor markets create chaotic disruptions and systemic injustices in the lives of poor people. Yet the creation and continuing existence of Maclovio Rojas demonstrates the simultaneous existence of counterhegemony. These women activists identify gaps and openings in the neoliberal system that make it possible for them to formulate new ideas and understandings of agency, autonomy, power, citizenship, and social membership. Active participation and leadership in collective campaigns for survival, subsistence, resistance, and affirmation have produced a woman-centered political subjectivity that challenges hegemonic ideals about national identity and belonging. We find autonomy in the spaces of neoliberal neglect.

By sharing the stories, thoughts, and experiences of Maclovianas, I have documented the ways in which these border women reject roles as "passive receivers of the transnational condition" (Escobar 2001, 155). Instead, they work actively to shape the terms of their lives. Through an analysis of the lived experiences of the *mujeres fronterizas* of Maclovio Rojas, I have illuminated how collective struggles on the border not only work to undo the dichotomous nature of women's public and private roles, but also make evident the border as a transformative space that can be hyperexploitative, given the transcendence of the nation-state by neoliberal logics, as well as a site where women come together to reimagine and redefine gendered, class-based, and racialized social structures.

The Possibilities of Transnational Organizing

The conditions in which communities find themselves living and working along the U.S.-Mexico border have ignited activist networks that transcend traditional political demarcations. This transnational—or transborder—activism has been identified by scholars as a significant collective response to globalization, creating networks that challenge inequalities in working conditions and environments produced by multinational corporations (Armbruster-Sandoval 2005; Bacon 2004; Bandy 2000; Bandy and Smith 2004; Keck and Sikking 1998; Liebowitz 2002; Staudt and Coronado 2002). Maclovio Rojas is embedded in a dense web of transnational relations. I find Gomez's (2016) definition of solidarity useful: "direct action and a political weapon, a form of praxis, a social tool, and a space of knowledge production. Solidarity can include but is not limited to direct aid, circulation of information about struggles, political interventions, and personal and organizational engagement with political movements in other countries" (9). A slow but steady stream of international visitors, invitations, and exchanges consistently come in and out of the community. I was there when Maclovianas/os received letters from Germany, Italy, and the United States, from activists, intellectuals, and ordinary workers and people who had learned about Maclovio Rojas and wanted to learn more from the residents.[1] All acknowledged the importance of their movement. Supporters and activists come to celebrate the community's annual anniversary in April by donating their time to perform, make food, and mark another year of existence.

Maclovio Rojas has received much support from U.S. church-based organizations that have sent volunteers to help construct homes, send food and supplies and organize toy drives during the holidays. However it's been the the innovative Border Arts Workshop/Taller de Arte Fronterizo (BAW/TAF), a binational (U.S./Mexico) group of artists formed in the late 1980s to work on issues of transculturality in the region and beyond, which has had

Figure 17. San Diego–based group Los Able Minded Poets perform at the sixteenth-anniversary celebration of the community. Michael Schnorr is in the frame carrying a camera. 2004.

a long-standing presence and impact in the community. Michael Schnorr was at the helm of many of these interventions from the mid-nineties until his death in 2012.[2] Over the course of many years, BAW/TAF artists and volunteers supported the building of much of the infrastructure to the community including the creation of the community center, the Aguascalientes, and even served on the general planning committee.[3] In addition, the BAW/TAF offered Saturday art classes to youth in the community who painted a number of impressive murals throughout Maclovio Rojas, documenting the oral histories of early women community members. These murals produce new public spaces. They turn blank walls into public representations of shared struggles. In the face of the pervasive power, reach, and scope of transnational media conglomerates and official educational institutions, the murals generate and display signs, symbols, and stories about local experiences and histories. The mural

Figure 18. "The well for water came from the moon when it flashed the women used a tarp as a glass and drank": mural that marks the early days of squatting, when the only water they had access to was from the rain. 2006.

Figure 19. Mural of Artemio Osuna and Hortensia Hernández behind bars by Elizabeth Huato. Photo by Oscar Michel. 2010.

Figure 20. A twenty-foot public archway with the negative space in the form of the Virgin of Guadalupe located near the cemetery. Artist: Judith Nicolaidis. Photo by Oscar Michel. 2010.

Figure 21. BAW/TAF offices on the side of the Aguascalientes with author and artist/activist Elizabeth Huato at the top of the stairs. 2004.

that is on the cover of this book was made in community but led by one of Schnorr's students, Elizabeth Huato.

Micro–radio programming came to the community through an organization called the Aztlan Media Collective, which created an opportunity not only for learning about radio programing, but also for transmitting their weekly experiences. John Martinez, a long-time activist and public media producer, made the drive from Los Angeles almost weekly to provide his support; he would stay in the upstairs loft at the Aguascalientes Community Center—an artists' residency space created by BAW/TAF.

These cross-border connections sometimes produce unique political opportunities. When Maclovio Rojas and the multinational corporation Hyundai were battling over land in 1997, the company might reasonably have expected itself to hold the upper hand in a fight with a small and impoverished border community. But BAW/TAF encouraged the publication of the article that appeared in the *Wall Street Journal* that listed eight powerful U.S. organizations that supported Maclovio Rojas. Hyundai Precision America, which had already appropriated one hundred acres, took notice and realized the fight with Maclovio Rojas was not going to be as easy as first imagined. Ted Chung, then president of Hyundai Precision America, stated, "We want to expand our factory if there's a reasonable timeline and cost. But we always see other opportunities. If the local people or local government can't let us do that, we can very easily change our plans and avoid the hardships. We could leave San Diego and Tijuana" (Laboy 1997). Soon after the article was published, Hyundai removed many of the cargo containers that had been the source of conflict between the company and the community. The uneven and differentiated social conditions on the two sides of the border—which draw multinational corporations to the region in the first place—made it possible for residents of Maclovio Rojas to recruit unexpected but powerful allies.

Maclovio Rojas has also supported binational collaboration and the creation of woman-centered spaces by offering space for meetings and events. In September 2004, the Colectiva Feminista Binacional (Téllez 2013) of San Diego/Tijuana organized an *encuentro*, or "gathering," with other activists working on issues affecting women in the border region. This was the first grassroots, binational, women-centered meeting hosted at the Maclovio Rojas women's center. The call for the encuentro stated: "Knowing each other gives us the opportunity to extend our own struggles and working together we can come up with strategies for better communication locally, regionally and bi-nationally. With this kind of gathering, we'll focus on the specific gendered problems that we face and, also, we will put forward a perspective from women and by women" (CFB event flyer 2004). In this encuentro the goals were to examine ties that already exist between organizations in Baja California, Mexico, and California, United States; to share different organizing experiences and learn from each other; to discuss solutions to the problems women workers, community members and organizers in this region face; to collectively reflect on their mutual identities; and to formulate strategies for support (2004).

The two-day gathering attracted over forty organizations from California and Baja California, as well as an organizer from Guatemala. It produced an unusual opportunity for conversation across national borders, class lines, and family formations. Encuentro participants included migrants, academics, students, union organizers, maquiladora workers, community health providers, Indigenous women, stay-at-home mothers, and members of the media. Considering that the gathering was organized and led by Maclovianas without any institutional support or external funding other than participant donations, the turnout was large and the event engaging and meaningful. It was at this meeting where important conversations and critical exchanges began to take place and the construction of a gendered *transfronteriza* cross-border collective identity to emerge and named as such (Téllez 2013).

Transnational flow also went in the other direction, to *el otro lado* and beyond, in two important ways—first, via the emails that the leadership sent out to their supporters. These communications allowed their stories and experiences to be transmitted, and, if immediate support was needed, it created an opportunity for outsiders to respond. Second, the film *Everyone Their Grain of Sand* (2004) transmitted the story of Maclovio Rojas internationally. The premiere was housed in the Centro Cultural de Tijuana (CECUT) the city's main center for the regional arts and one of the most important in the northwest of the country. But this opening day was unique, as the auditorium was filled with community members, Maclovianas/os who had left the poblado to participate in the premiere and watch as their story was shared. It was an important exchange, as the audience consisted of scholars, activists, and artists from both sides of the border interested in learning about the community. This film continues to circulate, and the story continues to be told, and as new generations become aware, new possibilities for transnational organizing emerge. Throughout their thirty-plus years of existence, these transnational collaborations have brought visibility to Maclovio Rojas.

In most written accounts, articles, and commentaries that I encountered, the leadership and presence of women is duly noted. This visibility has helped sustain the movement in times of great strain. I have also witnessed the inspiration that the women's strength gives to these collaborators, some having come from other parts of the world to learn from them. Given the violence that surrounds the community—both the structural violence enacted by the State and transnational companies and the physical violence that permeates border cities since the 2007 commencement of President Calderón's "War on Drugs"—Maclovio Rojas represents for many hope and possibility, or what Gonzalez (2020) calls "hope and imagination." While the women voice many frustrations, they also laugh as their everyday experiences of survival remind them to celebrate small feats: laughter as conviviality, laughter as solidarity, laughter as unity.

Figure 22. "The Community Center, Aguascalientes, is alive and kicking." 2016.

Esperanza and the Future of Maclovio Rojas

Many years ago I was told that the word *esperanza* (hope) derives from the word *esperar* (to wait). Linguistically this is incorrect, but the point of the observation was that, if one plans to have hope, one has to be prepared to wait. I think about the man who shared this with me from time to time, knowing full well that the system we live in, driven by the global market, drives many to hopelessness. The prospect of losing hope is a constant reality in Maclovio Rojas. In one of our conversations, Hortensia jokingly said that she foresaw the neoliberal state finding a way to charge for air, since every other natural resource now came with a price tag. We laughed as if this reality was completely implausible, but, given the disregard for the natural world by a global neoliberal economy—as seen, for example, in Bolivia, where Indigenous communities fought to retain their rights to water, or in North Dakota where Indigenous leaders from the

Standing Rock Nation battled the Dakota Access Pipeline (DAPL), and in the constant struggles for land that the story of Maclovio Rojas helps to highlight—deep down I think we both felt a tug of fear of what could actually come next.

Stahler-Sholk (2008) notes that autonomy is not a monolithic concept or a magic bullet against neoliberalism. Yet he also reminds us that community-controlled social and political institutions—schools, clinics, systems of justice, and regional planning—are an essential part of the struggle to define collective priorities independently of the logic of the market. Similarly, Andrea Smith (2008) has pointed out that we need to develop organizing models that are based on integrating political organizing into one's everyday life so that all people can participate. It is this organizing that makes Maclovio Rojas significant.

However, the commitment has its costs, as the demands can be overwhelming. In Maclovio Rojas I witnessed the toll activism took on the women—between hearings, clandestine meetings with Hortensia, consultations with the lawyers, asambleas in the community, and collective actions, it is not difficult to see that the challenges are great. At one point, Maria talked with me about needing a simple retreat, a possibility that is far removed from the day-in/day-out reality of women dedicated to her community. The likelihood of even one person taking a break is highly improbable, let alone the luxury of taking a group retreat. Dora made note of how this affects her personally: "Tengo mucha tensión, tengo mucha presión, estoy muy cansada" (I have a lot of tension, a lot of high blood pressure, I'm very tired), she explained, "No tienes tiempo para ti misma, a veces ni tenemos tiempo para comer" (You don't have time really for yourself, sometimes we don't have time to eat even). There were moments, particularly during Hortensia's exile, where the morale of the community was very low. In the six years of her physical absence she would send audio recordings and hold clandestine meetings with select leaders, but her presence was sorely missed. Feelings of being overwhelmed cannot easily be dismissed, and a solution isn't always visibly apparent. In this struggle, pausing even momentarily means risking an invasion by the government, risking that the infiltrators get control of another section—ultimately, risking everything you have. Taking a break is just not an option. Instead, hope and the vision for change keep the Maclovianas moving forward collectively.

The experiences of women on the frontlines of the land battle in Maclovio Rojas illuminate emerging practices of citizenship, belonging, and community-building in a region shaped by the global economic system and characterized by the stark contrasts between wealth and poverty. The effectiveness of their grassroots organizing, as witnessed in their community formation, provides an alternative to the kinds of politics permitted by neoliberal nation states. The colonia declares the legitimacy of its autonomous identity by invoking a now-repealed section of the Mexican Constitution. But, while not really supported by the letter of the law, the appeal to the promises made by the Mexican Revolution give the efforts of Maclovio Rojas a sense of legitimacy in their own eyes, as well as in the eyes of others. It is the failure of the Mexican state to provide needed services that compels the residents of Maclovio Rojas to provide for themselves.

Political mobilization in Maclovio Rojas also differs markedly from the forms of self-activity and governance promoted by transnational nongovernmental agencies and organizations. As Dohlinow (2010) argues, the NGOs think of leadership and governance in entrepreneurial terms, as an individualistic self-serving enterprise that relieves the state of responsibility for supporting everyone by allowing the most organized sectors of the poor to make gains at the expense of unorganized. The ideal of empowerment that has emerged from the struggles of Maclovio Rojas revolves around a model of solidarity and collectivity that points the way toward progressive social change for society as a whole. In the process of challenging corporations, governments, and transnational agencies and institutions, activism generates new social subjects and subjectivities, new identities and new identifications. The women-centered political subjectivity guiding this produces not only new individual leaders, but also new understandings of leadership as collective, transformative, and accountable. Leadership in the public sphere is not juxtaposed against activities in the private sphere; instead, putatively personal needs become linked with political practices to transform both individual and group identities. In the act of speaking back to power, women find new voices capable of calling a community into being and carrying its concerns and claims to wider audiences. Through their praxis, the border becomes not just a locus of migration and marginalization but also a site that generates new forms of organization and mobilization.

I concur with Peña (2007), who argues that success in women's mobilizations should not be measured primarily in terms of success in mobilizing material resources or moving in vast networks. Rather, many marginalized peoples' success lies more in moving women to greater action in both public and private spheres. Because economic

Figure 23. Looking northwest at the crosses that line the perimeter of the cemetery in honor of those migrants who have died crossing the border. 2005.

marginality and domestic centrality leave women especially vulnerable to the depredations of neoliberalism, constructing a counterhegemony entails renegotiating the terms of the gendered division of labor and reward. The constraints that women face are not only political and economic, but also cultural and familial (Moghadam 2001). The continuing consequences of the coloniality of power and the constant generation of new forms of racialized and gendered inequalities require women in Maclovio Rojas to develop forms of struggle that challenge patriarchy and racialization at the same time that they fight the State and transnational companies.

Although the goals of Maclovio Rojas residents revolve around the struggle for land, an important by-product of that struggle is the emergence of a woman-centered political consciousness that can be replicated elsewhere. In the course of gaining the capacity to shape the decisions that affect their life chances, Maclovianas learn new ways to live. In the act of creating safe spaces for themselves and for their families, these mujeres fronterizas take an oppositional stance toward the State, transnational corporations, and patriarchy. In the process, they prove that change in all aspects of a woman's life is possible. As Hortensia said to me, "Todo lo que existe nos pertenece a todas/os" (Everything that exists belongs to us all).

Closing Thoughts

My journey as a scholar-activist brought me to this work, to this place in the borderlands where I grew up, that eventually placed me on the trajectory to write this book. I concur with Veronica Gago's (2020) notion that there is a very close relationship between knowledge production and political practice. I continue to find it imperative that we recognize the borderlands as a space of conviviality, community formation and creative and collective exchange—experiences that are shaped by woman-centered political subjectivity. I mentioned my friend Nacho at the beginning—we've remained close, even though almost twenty-five years have passed since my initial contact with the Movimiento Autónomo in Madrid. I saw him in Barcelona in 2018, where we talked about the evolution of his initial work as an autonomist youth that led him to form part of one of the most progressive governments in the city of Madrid: Ahora Madrid. Once the Centro Social Seco became part of the municipality and was moved into a brand-new location, there was a rupture between those who wanted to remain autonomous and those who were finding ways to work within the city structure—hoping to effect change in some key local issues and practices. The tensions between strategies and scope might not need to be seen as such. I'm reminded of Nacho's point that it takes more time to build than to destroy. As Holloway (2019) says, while we "urgently need to change the world radically, it cannot be done through the state, [however], changing it without taking state power is very difficult" (8). And yet people continue to envision more liberatory futures.

There is the town of Marinaleda, a community in Andalusia, in southern Spain, with a population of about 2,700, whose mayor, Sánchez Gordillo, has worked toward creating the future in the present—autonomous, with its own farmland and governmental structure. Some would argue that, after close to forty years since its inception, Marinaleda has more stability compared to the rest of the country (Hancox 2013). In 1991, residents won the El Humoso farm, which gave them 1200 hectares of land; instead of fighting against the State, they've been able to build toward a cooperative economic structure that seems to be benefiting the town's population.

In September 2020, nineteen families purchased ninety-six acres of land to create a safe haven for Black people in the U.S. state of Georgia. Cofounders Ashley Scott and Renee Walter describe it as a self-contained Black community. "It's now time for us to get our friends and family together and build for ourselves," said Walters, who serves as the president of the organization. "That's the only way we'll be safe. And that's the only way that this will work. We have to start bringing each other together" (Francis and Newton 2020).[4] What would it mean if the residents of Maclovio Rojas had been allowed to bring their projects to fruition without the constant threat of attack, theft and criminalization?

My daughter is now fifteen years old. The last time she was in Maclovio Rojas, she was ten. I remember her running through the community, picking up our favorite snack at the tiendita (Tostilocos) and reconnecting with some of her old friends. I'm not sure what she'll remember of this experience as she journeys into adulthood. I've thought deeply about how I want to create the world we want now for her and our future generations. Enacting prefigurative politics means behaving in the day-to-day as much as possible

Figure 24. Hortensia Hernández stands in front of the Aguascalientes with her son and my daughter. 2016.

in the way that you envision new social and economic relationships. Maclovio Rojas is certainly one response of creating new ways of being when the system hasn't served us (Grise 2017). In the absence of a territory, in the absence of a land base, in the absence, really, of a national identity—or, better said, in the absence of an attachment to a nation-state as Chicanx—I do believe that the transformation I imagine must begin in our relationships, in our homes, in our communities, in our reconnection to our ancestral ways. These are the practices that I consider in my role as a mother, community member, and educator. My hope is to deepen the grietas of creation resistance as we connect them in order to further unravel the layered systems of domination and capital.

I think back to one of my most favorite memories: the evenings in Maclovio Rojas. The noise from the highway seems to dim, the dust appears to settle, and the sun sets right behind the mountains that overlook the community. Tranquility envelops the community and the families, who are living on the little plots of land that they set out to find and on which to build a simple life, enjoying what they have most struggled for: a place to call home in the borderlands.

EPILOGUE

FELIPE CALDERON BECAME PRESIDENT OF Mexico in 2006 (2006–12), and while he continued to expand neoliberal politics, he also left a horrific legacy of violence and forced disappearances through his nationally touted "war on drugs" campaign.[1] During this time, hundreds of thousands of people have been killed or disappeared in Mexico. I do not write about this time period, because when I returned to Maclovio Rojas in 2016 (my last visit had been in 2010), the leadership did not discuss the impact on the community—perhaps it was old news by the time I reappeared, or perhaps it was just another obstacle among hundreds that they have had to face as a community. In all honesty, the violence in Tijuana is what kept me away for a few years, yet somehow I felt like I had betrayed them if I admitted that (because if I didn't feel safe in a place they lived, how did I truly accompany them?); I, too, didn't ask directly about that time period. In 2016, Hortensia was back in the community, as was Nicolasa—they were no longer targeted by the State in the same way and could move about freely. Hortensia and her partner had adopted a little boy and she was still focused on getting titles for the land as the residents of the community continued to build on their visions. Enrique Peña Nieto was now president (2012–18) and the PRI was back in power, yet the national political landscape did nothing to change the predicament of the community.

As I prepared this manuscript and continued to do research, however, I discovered an awful truth about the community. From 2006 until today, the geography of many border cities have been reconfigured by *narco* (drug) violence—the shootings, the roadblocks, the mutilated bodies were uncovered time and time again. In response, we were all forced to learn a new language to be able to describe the realities unfolding before us, like "narco graves" and "safe houses"—however, "pozolero" was one I had yet to learn about:

> Pozole is a popular Mexican stew that can feature pork, hominy and an array of vegetables and seasonings. But the name of the delicacy has taken on a sinister new meaning: Mexican authorities have detained a man linked to hundreds of deaths in the drug war who is being called the Pozole Maker. The man, Santiago Meza López, known as "el Pozolero" in the Mexican news media, has confessed to dissolving the remains of 300 people in acid while working for a top drug trafficker, the Mexican Army said Friday. Dissolving bodies is gaining increasing popularity in the internecine killings between rival traffickers that is playing out here, and the practice has become known as making pozole (pronounced poh-ZOH-leh). (*New York Times* 2009)

It took another three years before they were able to identify the location of the mass grave that "El Pozolero" had created—located in Maclovio Rojas, the lot was known as "La gallera" (chicken coop). El pozolero had tipped off the location, and after the ineptitude of the local police, Fernando Ocegueda, president of the civil association United for the Disappeared of Baja California and father of a young man who was disappeared, began the search for the property known as La Gallera. For two years, on weekends, they searched this area in

Maclovio Rojas until, at the end of 2012, the mass grave was found. Let me emphasize that it was not the State that opened an investigation to search for and identify these graves (Ovalle, Díaz Tovar, and Ongay 2014). Even in death, the State denies *el Mexico profundo*. This, too, is autonomy.

Where does this leave Maclovianos? How do you make sense of this violence in one's community? Is it possible to repair the social fabric lost after uncovering this kind of truth? The resilient residents of Maclovio Rojas collectively decided to recover the property and turn it into a community space. Ovalle et al. (2014), who were part of the creation of this space, write:

> As authors of this work, we saw the graffiti on the walls that said "an eye for an eye" and "we don't play games." We were at the meetings where they [the residents] discussed their fears but they made the decision not to give up in the face of fear. Some of the comments we recorded said: "We don't want problems with nobody, but we can't leave that place there, buried, forgotten, like something dark and sad in our community" and "The most bad, something good can come out, we already lost a generation of young people who left us for the narco path, now that this place reminds you that this is not an option." Their objective and quest was clear: to face fear and work for the reconstruction of your community. (290)

In February 2014, after many meetings and discussions between relatives of the victims, residents of the community, and the team of researchers and documentarians from the Institute of UABC-Museum Cultural Research and Visual Anthropology Studies, the community inaugurated a museum: Place of Remembrance and Reconciliation. The main objective of this intervention was to respond to the request of the next of kin of the victims, who had been demanding that this place become a memorial. It also answered the need of the neighbors, who had called for "a transformation of the energies of this place"—from a dark and gloomy setting into a space for life, hope, and memory. According to those who were present at the inauguration, Hortensia said some words at the opening. Moved by the result, she thanked the university and said that she had never imagined that, from those ruins that the community wanted to bury, "something good for Maclovio" could resurface. In collaboration with local artists and universities, moreover, various art installations memorialized the victims. In essence, the space was resignified and became a space of hope; it seems that esperanza once again regained its place as a recurring theme in Maclovio Rojas.

I last communicated with Hortensia in March 2021, when I showed her what would become the cover for this book. She sent me a message on Facebook:

Me removiste mi corazón. Fue triste, amargo, porque por años fuí perseguida por políticos policiacos. Sin ser delincuente, mi delito fue por buscar una vida, educación, salud, deporte digno. Pero valió la pena, hoy se han beneficiado más de 12,000 habitantes, y me siento contenta que mis compañeros y yo salimos casi triunfantes porque ahora nos falta nuestros títulos de nuestra propiedad. Y gracias Michel [sic] porque tú formaste parte de nuestra vida tan marginada y nos apoyaste a salir adelante. Te queremos mucho. Y esta portada me removió pero también me hizo reflexionar y pensar con satisfacción que valió la pena.

(You stirred my heart. It was sad, bitter, because for years I was persecuted by police and politicians. Without being a criminal, my crime was to seek a dignified life, education, health, sport. But it was worth it, today more than 12,000 inhabitants have benefited, and I am happy that my *compañeros* and I came out almost triumphant as we await the titles of our property. And thank you, Michel [sic], for you were part of our marginalized and you supported us to get ahead. We love you very much. And this cover moved me, but it also made me reflect and think with satisfaction that it was worth it.)

Selected Glossary

ASAMBLEAS: community meetings

AUTONOMÍA: autonomy

CAMPESINOS: farmers

CHISPA: a spark

COLONIAS: unregulated subdivisions

COLONOS: residents/community members

CONCIENTIZAR: to raise consciousness

COORDINADORAS: autonomous governing bodies

DESPOJO: land occupation

EJIDOS: communal lands

ENCUENTRO: intentional gathering

EN LUCHA: in struggle

GOLPE: hit, attempted overthrow

GRANJAS: family farms

JEFAS DE MANZANA: block coordinators

LOTES COMERCIALES: roadside commercial lots

MANDADOS: errands

MAQUILADORA: border factories

MÁS ENTRONAS: more daring

MEXICANIDAD: Mexicanness

MEXICO PROFUNDO: deep Mexico

MUJERES FRONTERIZAS: border women

MUNICIPIOS: municipalities

NARCO: drug trafficker

OKUPAS: alternative social and cultural centers; squatter movement

POBLADO: land settlement/community

SEXENIO: the six-year presidential term of office

SOBRE-RUEDAS: farmers markets

TERRENO: plot of land

LA VIVIENDA: home or dwelling

Notes

Prologue

1. The *Okupa* (squatter) movement was very popular in Western Europe in the late 1980s and 1990s. Usually, abandoned buildings were "taken over" by youth and turned into thriving autonomous cultural and political centers. By the late 1990s, many of these centers had been shut down by local police. However, I returned to Madrid in the early 2000s and made a short documentary about the status of the *centro social* in the community of Vallecas that I had learned so much from and in: see "Centro Social Seco," November 10, 2011, https://vimeo.com/31925044. As I'll discuss in the conclusion, this particular movement proved to outlive many others.

2. I use *asamblea* throughout this book to both convey the gatherings and community meetings held in Maclovio Rojas and to signify it as an example of an autonomous and participatory practice of self-governance.

3. Our binational organizing work in support of the Zapatistas had created many moments of exchange. For example, in March 1999, the Zapatistas organized La Consulta (the plebiscite) on Indigenous rights and culture, in order to pressure the government into implementing the signed San Andres accords. The Zapatistas sent one man and one woman (five thousand civilian Zapatistas in total) to every municipality in the country. They came to the city of Tijuana, and I was able to visit with them and participate in the action at the U.S.-Mexico border along with helping to organize the ballots for La Consulta. The

idea was to get the vote of all Mexicans, including those living in the United States and abroad. Our coalition, led by the San Diego–based organization Union del Barrio, set up ballot boxes in Barrio Logan, Chicano Park, in San Diego, California. On March 21 of the same year, three million Mexicans voted to demand the implementation of the San Andres Accords to no avail. For more information, see "Zapatista Timeline," Schools for Chiapas, https://schoolsforchiapas.org/teach-chiapas/zapatista-timeline (accessed March 11, 2021).

4. I created a documentary about the caravan: "Amor y Resistencia," posted October 1, 2013, https://vimeo.com/49260484.

5. Center Plaza in México City.

6. We also visited the Casa de la Cultura Benito Juarez, another autonomous social space, created and organized by youth, in one of the poorest barrios in east Mexico City: Iztapalapa.

7. To learn more about the transnational support activities between Zapatista and Chicana/o/x communities in the United States, see Martha Gonzalez (2020), Pablo Gonzalez (2011), Xochi Flores (2020), and Roberto Gonzalez Flores (2008).

8. On January 1, 1996, the Ejercito Zapatista de Liberacion Nacional called for the creation of the Frente Zapatista de Liberacion Nacional (FZLN), a national civil Zapatista organization that would build a new kind of political movement. This new organization would be built from the ground up by citizens committed to carrying out Zapatista political principles such as *mandar obedeciendo*, or "rule by obeying." Instead of being a vanguard that would represent the masses, the FZLN was to become the collector and organizer of the people's proposals (Zugman 2005).

9. In August 1994, the Zapatistas convened the National Democratic Convention to open a national dialogue with "civil society." To host six thousand participants, they built an auditorium like a giant ark with a white canvas roof in a community they renamed "Aguascalientes," to invoke the convention held in that city in Central México during the 1910 Revolution. More auditoriums appeared throughout the country among Indigenous communities in resistance. In 1996, the Zapatistas made a call to international civil society to establish multiple Aguascalientes in order to host cultural, political and social exchanges. In August 2003, the EZLN announced the closure of the Aguascalientes and a shift from autonomous municipalities to Caracoles, which would be the "Casas" de la Junta de Buen Gobierno (Homes of the Good Government).

10. My initial plan was to live in the community for the course of the year, but, due to the aggressions of the state and the subsequent exile of the community leaders, my advisor and department at the time would not permit my living there.

11. All of the interviews with Maclovianas quoted throughout were conducted by the author between 2003 and 2016, unless otherwise noted.

12. I use "State" when referring to or wanting to convey the assemblages of power that are the confluence of federal, local, and multinational systems of power.

13. I'm building on the long Latin American tradition of *testimoniando* as oppositional knowledge. *Testimonio* is a story that is told from a place of intent and understanding of social, political, and historical contexts and oppositional consciousness (see Delgado Bernal, Burciaga, and Flores Carmona 2012; Latina Feminist Group 2001). I'm also grateful to the Center for Convivial Research and Autonomy (http://ccra.mitotedigital.org/ccra) for building on Latina Feminist Group's use of testimonio to theorize oppression, resistance, and subjectivity by highlighting the notion of collaborative or relational testimonio. This is a theoretical tool that marks the coconstruction, the coarchiving, and collaborative circulation of unique knowledges of struggle.

14. All names are pseudonyms, except for Hortensia's; her real name appears throughout this book at her request.

15. In my other work, I use the concept of politicized transfronteriza identity to further describe the movements of transborder solidarity that emerged in support of maquiladora workers (Téllez 2013).

16. I was struggling to make sense of my academic and community commitments, a tension I later embraced and wrote about in my first published article, "Doing Research at the Borderlands: Notes from a Chicana Feminist Ethnographer" (Téllez 2005).

Introduction

1. As Esteva (2001) argues, "autonomy" has a long tradition in the popular movements in Mexico. The struggle for university autonomy in the 1920s created a chorus of meanings and connotations that reappeared in the 1970s and joined naturally with the expression of civil society. Magaña (2020) further points out that "any study of contemporary movements for autonomy in Latin America must position those

struggles in relation to the surge in Indigenous and Afro-descendant social movements that started in the late 1980s and 1990s" (61).

2. Since the 1994 uprising and the failed 1997 San Andrés Accords talks, the Zapatistas have maintained control over their territories and governed them autonomously from government intrusion.

3. See Gaspar Rivera, Lynn Stephens, and Jonathan Fox, "Indigenous Rights and Self-Determination in Mexico," *Cultural Survival Quarterly* (March 1999): https://www.culturalsurvival.org/publications/cultural-survival-quarterly/indigenous-rights-and-self-determination-México (accessed April 16, 2021).

4. See Clayton Conn, "Mexico: Guerrero's Indigenous Community Police and Self-defense Groups," Upside Down World, March 4, 2013, https://upsidedownworld.org/archives/mexico/mexico-guerreros-indigenous-community-police-and-self-defense-groups/.

5. When referencing women from Maclovio Rojas I will use *Maclovianas*; if I am discussing the entire community, I will use *Maclovianas/os*, as the community members do.

6. Oscar Martínez (1994) defines the greater borderlands as "the U.S. and Mexican border states –Texas, New Mexico, Arizona, and California on the American side and Tamaulipas, Nuevo León, Coahuila, Chihuahua, Sonora, and Baja California on the Mexican side" (40–41). As Callahan (2003) notes and expands, "The important aspect to be noted here is the interdependence and ultimately the coherence of the region" (x).

7. In *Caliban and the Witch* (2004), Federici shows that "the body has been for women in capitalist society what the factory has been for male waged workers: the primary ground of their exploitation and resistance, as the female body has been appropriated by the state and men and forced to function as a means for the reproduction and accumulation of labor" (16).

8. Please also see Sayak Valencia's theory of "gore capitalism" that further highlights these assemblages of power at the border through a lens that includes organized crime as a necessary embodiment of hegemonic and global economic processes that increase radical violence and produces death as a commodity.

9. Also see Castells (1996).

10. *Buen vivir* or *vivir bien* (the good life) are the Spanish words used in Latin America to describe alternatives to development focused on the good life in a broad sense. The term is actively used by social movements, and it has become popular in some government programs. The richness of the term is difficult to translate into English; it includes the

classical ideas of quality of life, but with the specific idea that well-being is only possible within a community. Furthermore, in most approaches the community concept is understood in an expanded sense, to include nature. *Buen vivir* therefore embraces the broad notion of well-being and cohabitation with others and Nature (Gudynas 2011).

11. I acknowledge the contribution of Devon G. Peña for suggesting this combination of the minimalist welfare and maximalist surveillance and security state formation. He first proposed this idea in the MexMigration blog in May 2010; for the original post, see "The State of Exception, Capital, and Private Property," http://mexmigration.blogspot .com/2010/06/arizona-challenging-state-of-exception_28.html?q= arizona+challenging+state+of+exception (accessed March 20, 2021).

12. While I didn't have the language when I began this research, Abrego's (2020) notion of research as accompaniment is useful here: "Instead, we are deeply committed to people's wellbeing just as much as, and often more than, to the advancement of a field. We are aiming to be in accompaniment" (3).

13. *Cada uno su granito de arena* is a popular phrase in Mexico that essentially describes cooperation; it is also the name of a film about Maclovio Rojas (translated to "Everyone their grain of sand") made by filmmaker Elizabeth "Beth" Bird (1966–2021). Released in 2004, the film premiered at the main Cultural Arts Center (CECUT) in Tijuana in November of that year; it was a huge success because the organizers wanted to make sure that the residents of the community were present in a space that was typically inaccessible to them. The city clearly took note. Following the event, one headline read "Abarrotan maclovianos el Cecut" (Maclovianos cram into Cecut); see https://insiteart.org/uploads/files/El -Sol-de-Tijuana-November-22-2004.pdf?fbclid=IwAR2pMCkqMVra _YgxaImSw5vyxBNpA-fYyTES7_ZRep2CMI6w8ICz9BeqHOU (accessed April 22, 2021).

Chapter 1

1. CIOAC stands for Central Independiente de Obreros Agrígolas y Campesinos, a farmworkers union that had a history of organizing migrant Mixteco farm workers in the tomato fields in the state of Sinaloa, and in San Quintín, Baja California, south of Tijuana.

2. According to the research currently being conducted by University of California, San Diego (UCSD), history PhD student Jorge Ramirez,

the death of Maclovio Rojas led to a corrido composed in honor of his contributions to the San Quintín farmworker struggle. Please see "From the Fields to the Struggle for Home: Temporary Workers and Indigenous Farm Worker Self-Activity in an Incipient Export Agricultural Region, 1984–1990," in his forthcoming dissertation, "Becoming Indigenous: Race, Violence, and Indigeneity between Southern Mexico and the U.S.-Mexican Pacific Coast, 1970–1994."

3. April 10 is also the anniversary of México's revolutionary hero Emiliano Zapata's death in 1919. This is a symbolic origin story residents often mention, linking their movement to a longer history of land struggle and reform in México.

4. Residents no longer fight over the plots of land disputed with Hyundai. Today the company employs approximately three thousand people, many even from Maclovio Rojas. In 2014, they inaugurated an adjacent plant.

5. Though the point of departure of this book begins postindependence, I recognize that all land is unceded Indigenous territory. See Roberto D. Hernandez's book (2018) for a history of the Kumeyaay/Tipai-Ipai nations in the region I focus on.

6. These would be the first actually competitive presidential elections in Mexico since the (PRI) took power in 1929. In all previous presidential elections, the PRI had faced no serious opposition and had won with percentages of votes well over 70 percent. Although early results of the parallel vote tabulation had indicated Cuauhtémoc Cárdenas was winning, when the official results were announced, Salinas was said to have eked out a narrow victory. A 2019 study in the American Political Science Review found "evidence of blatant alterations" in approximately one third of the tallies in the election.

7. The nation-building discourses of mestizaje or "Imaginary México" reframed the colonial and racial markers of largely poor Indigenous and mestizo populations (Mexico profundo) into the language of "peasants" as part of its attempt to create illusion that colonial situations were over.

8. As dictated by the community, not state-recognized titles.

9. Dalla Costa and James (1972) have been making this point since the seventies.

Chapter 2

1. Interviewed by author in October 2003.

2. This same script was followed by anyone running the Platica for the week.

3. Fraccion III del articulo 226 del Codigo Penal del Estado. Maclovio Rojas fact sheet, prepared by Globalifobic@s, 2002.

4. Please see David Harvey's (2003) discussion on primitive accumulation where land is taken and enclosed and resident populations are expelled "to create a landless proletariat, and then releasing the land into the privatised mainstream of capital accumulation through violence, war, enslavement, and colonialism" (149).

5. In the 1930s, this was called the "Great Repatriation," and later, in the 1950s, as a result of continued nativism and racialized scapegoating, the program returned under the name "Operation Wetback" (Mirande 1987).

6. Population Dynamics, United Nations. Department of Economic and Social Affairs, 2018, https://worldpopulationreview.com/world-cities/tijuana-population (accessed March 31, 2021).

7. I just want to note that while Hortensia discussed her Indigenous roots and cosmologies, the majority of the residents did not identify as such. Although many of the early reports of the movement classify the community as Indigneous or Mixteco (Oaxacan), this is not simply the case. I analyzed the list of residents and their region of origins, and the majority—if not all—of residents do not identify as Indigenous and are from northern states.

8. And, more recently, Central Americans—although this shift happened after my fieldwork, it would be interesting to return to note the changes.

9. By using the term "commons" I am drawing on a long tradition that is best understood through a feminist lens. Federici (2012) argues that "a feminist perspective on the commons is important because it begins with the realization that, as the primary subjects of reproductive work, historically and in our time, women have depended on access to communal natural resources more than men and have been most penalized by their privatization and most committed to their defense" (n.p.).

Chapter 3

1. The first part of this chapter title, "Social Transformation in the Present," borrows from the article "Reproducción comunitaria de la vida:

Pensando la trans-formación social en el presente" in the Mexican journal *El Apantle: Revista de Estudios Comunitarios*, by Gutiérrez and Salazar Lohman (2015).

2. While names suggest lots of splintering, each is important in their own right and speaks to specificity of each struggle and project.

3. In the last few years, she's had a street named after her in the community. When I asked Hortensia about it, she said, "The community decided to put my name after I left the Tijuana penitentiary [El Pueblito de la Mesa], that's what they called this place. I asked them to wait until I died, if they wanted to put my name somewhere. But they decided, that, no, in life."

4. The Aguascalientes was inaugurated on July 4, 1998, to commemorate the 11th anniversary of Maclovio Rojas's death.

5. Small business owners (e.g., restaurants).

6. I will discuss the role of BAW/TAF in the conclusion.

7. This project took almost thirteen years to complete; it ended up not going through the community directly but was not too far. The high-speed highway has created other problems in the city—namely, an increased number of highway deaths. Juan Miguel Hernandez, "A 13 años de su inauguración, el bulevar 2000 de Tijuana es peligro sin fin," *El Sol de Tijuana*, August 4, 2019, https://www.lavozdelafrontera.com .mx/local/a-13-anos-de-su-inauguracion-el-bulevar-2000-de-tijuana-es -peligro-sin-fin-3991254.html.

8. Between 1995 and 2002, Hortensia was detained three times and spent a year in prison. She lived in hiding between 2002 and 2008.

9. *Compañera/o* is a difficult word to translate; it could mean "comrade" or "companion," but *compañera/o* conveys specifically the idea of accompaniment, which, as I see it, is also solidarity in action.

Chapter 4

1. I understand the polemic regarding the politics of recognition and the argument by Coulthard (2014) that one doesn't need the state for recognition, and that, in fact, the state maintains both the objective and subjective realms of colonial power. This is the productive tension that Maclovianos constantly negotiate in their movement and that I document throughout this book.

2. See Magaña (2020) for an important ethnography of the 2006 generation in Oaxaca; his work gives new meanings to comunalidad, autonomy, and youth culture in urban spaces.

3. While Maclovianas use the term *reconocimiento*, I draw from Goett's (2016) work in Monkey Point, Nicaragua, which shows the radical potential and force behind Black autonomy that is not premised on recognition but stems from "intimate spheres of social life" (6). In these everyday spheres of "self-valorization, community people draw on a reservoir of political knowledge and oppositional subjectivity grounded in a shared Black diasporic experience and gendered cultural practices. Black autonomy as an achieved state is a utopian aspiration given the racial violence and compromised political conditions that community people must negotiate on a daily basis. But Black autonomy does exist as a real and vibrant social practice rooted in working-class Creole culture that is resistant to racial hierarchies and capitalist values even as it sometimes remains in contradictory tension with patriarchy" (185).

4. School code, which signifies that the government has sanctioned the school.

5. Thank you to Cynthia Bejarano for helping me make this connection.

6. Artemio was vice president of the community for many years, until there was a break in the leadership. Hortensia remains the elected and recognized leader of the community.

7. Juan is Nicolasa Ramos's partner; she was incarcerated for three years for allegedly stealing water.

Conclusion

1. This stream of supporters was documented in the early years by artist Manuel Mancillas (2001): "BAW facilitates solidarity and working delegations to the Poblado. The Orange County Friends of Maclovio Rojas through fundraising purchased a towing trailer to transport garage doors and building materials. The American Friends Service Committee sends annual delegations from their youth program for a week-long stay for community work projects. Global Exchange also brings a youth program. Recently, two French scholars spent a 6 week long residency in the center producing a documentary for French TV. An Australian graduate student is working on a performance-based

research project; and a Brazilian artist is developing a summer-long residency and community event planned for this year."

2. A wealth of information exists about the work of BAW/TAF in general and in Maclovio Rojas in the Michael Schnorr Collection of Border Art Workshop/Tallér de Arte Fronterízo Records, 1978–2008, held at the UCSD Library Special Collections and Archives.

3. Artist Tanya Aguiñiga details some of this history here: https://www.craftinamerica.org/short/tanya-aguiniga-on-the-history-of-maclovio-rojas-mexico (accessed April 16, 2021).

4. Marquise Francis and Kamilah Newton, "19 Black Families Purchase 96 Acres of Land to Create a 'Safe Haven' for Black People," Yahoo! News, September 3, 2020, https://news.yahoo.com/19-black-families-purchased-96-acres-of-land-to-create-a-safe-haven-for-black-people-215152697.html.

Epilogue

1. Sayak Valencia's (2018) theory of "gore capitalism" is again useful in understanding how death becomes a source of surplus value; gore capitalism refers to the explicit and unjustified bloodletting that occurs along the Mexican border.

References

Abrego, L. 2021. "Research as Accompaniment: Reflections on Objectivity, Ethics, and Emotions." In *Out of Place: Power, Person, and Difference in Socio-Legal Research*, edited by Lynnette Chua and Mark Massoud. Accessed April 22, 2021. https://escholarship.org/uc/item/34v2g837.

Abu-Lughod, Lila. 1991. "Writing Against Culture." In *Recapturing Anthropology: Working in the Present*, edited by Richard G. Fox, 137–62. Santa Fe: School of American Research Press.

Adler-Hellman, Judith. 1994. *Mexican Lives*. New York: New Press.

Adler-Hellman, Judith. 2008. "Mexican Popular Movements, Clientelism, and the Process of Democratization." In *Latin American Social Movements in the Twenty-First Century: Resistance, Power, and Democracy*, edited by Richard Stahler-Sholk, Harry E. Vanden, and Glen David Kuecker, 61–76. Lanham, Md.: Rowman & Littlefield.

Agamben, Giorgio. 2005. *State of Exception*. Chicago: University of Chicago Press.

Agarwal, Bina. 1995. "Research and Policy Questions on Women and Land Rights." Submission to Gender-Prop E-mail Conference. September 20, 1995. Washington, D.C.: International Food Policy Research Institute.

Aguilar, Carolina, and Alicia Chenard. 1994. "Is There a Place for Feminism in the Revolution?" In *Compañeras: Voices from the Latin American*

Women's Movement, edited by Gabby Kuppers, 102–10. London: Latin American Bureau.

Aida Hernandez Castillo, Rosalva. 2016. *Multiple Injustices: Indigenous Women, Law, And Political Struggle in Latin America*. Tucson: University of Arizona Press.

Andreas, Peter. 2000. *Border Games: Policing the U.S.-Mexico Divide*. Ithaca, N.Y.: Cornell University Press.

Anzaldúa, Gloria. 1987. *Borderlands/La Frontera: The New Mestiza*. San Francisco: Aunt Lute.

Armbruster-Sandoval, Ralph. 2005. "Workers of the World Unite? The Contemporary Anti-Sweatshop Movement and the Struggle for Social Justice in the Americas." *Work and Occupations* 32: 464–85.

Arroyo, Alberto P. 2003. "Promesas y realidades: El Tratado de Libre Comercio de América del Norte en su noveno año." *Revista Venezolana de Economía y Ciencias Sociales* 9: 167–95.

Audley, John, Demetrios Papademetriou, Sandra Polaski, and Scott Vaughan. 2003. *NAFTA's Promise and Reality: Lessons from Mexico for the Hemisphere*. Washington, D.C.: Carnegie Endowment for International Peace.

Baca Zinn, Maxine. 1979. "Field Research in Minority Communities: Ethical, Methodological, and Political Observations by an Insider." *Social Problems* 27, no. 2: 209–19.

Bacon, David. 2004. *The Children of NAFTA: Labor Wars on the U.S./Mexico Border*. Berkeley: University of California Press.

Bakker, Karen. 2007. "The 'Commons' Versus the 'Commodity': Alter-Globalization, Anti-Privatization, and the Human Right to Water in the Global South." *Antipode* 39: 450–55.

Bandy, Joe. 2000. "Bordering the Future: Resisting Neoliberalism in the Borderlands." *Critical Sociology* 26: 232–67.

Bandy, Joe, and Jackie Smith, eds. 2004. *Coalitions Across Borders: Transnational Protest and the Neoliberal Order*. Lanham, Md.: Rowman & Littlefield.

Bandy, Joe, and Jennifer B. Mendez. 2006. "A Place of Their Own? Women Organizers in the Maquilas of Mexico and Nicaragua." In *Latin American Social Movements: Globalization, Democratization, and Transnational Networks*, edited by Hank Johnson and Paul Almeida, 131–46. Lanham, Md.: Rowman & Littlefield.

Barros Nock, Magdalena. 2000. "The Mexican Peasantry and the Ejido in the Neo-Liberal Period." In *Disappearing Peasantries? Rural Labour in Africa, Asia, and Latin America*, edited by Deborah Bryceson, Cristobal Kay, and Jos Mooji, 332–44. London: Intermediate Technology.

Barton, Carol. 2004. "Global Women's Movements at a Crossroads: Seeking Definition, New Alliances and Greater Impacts." *Socialism and Democracy* 18: 151–84.

Behar, Ruth. 1993. *Translated Woman: Crossing the Border with Esperanza's Story*. Boston: Beacon.

Bejarano, Cynthia L. 2002. "Las Super Madres de Latino America: Transforming Motherhood by Challenging Violence in Mexico, Argentina, and El Salvador." *Frontiers: A Journal of Women's Studies* 23, no. 1: 126–50.

Bennett, Vivienne. 1992. "The Evolution of the Popular Movements in Mexico Between 1968 and 1988." In *The Making of Social Movements in Latin America: Identity, Strategy, and Democracy*, edited by Arturo Escobar and Sonia Alvarez, 240–59. Boulder, Colo.: Westview.

Bhavnani, Kum-Kum, John Foran, and Priya Kurian, eds. 2003. *Feminist Futures: Re-imagining Women, Culture and Development*. London: Zed.

Bickham Mendez, Jennifer. 2005. *From the Revolution to the Maquiladoras: Gender, Labor and Globalization in Nicaragua*. Durham, N.C.: Duke University Press.

Blackwell, Maylei. 2004. "(Re) Ordenando el Discurso de la Nación: El Movimiento de Mujeres Indígenas en Mexico y la Práctica de la Autonomía." In *Mujeres y nacionalismo: De la Independencia a la Nación del Nuevo Milenio*, edited by Natividad Gutiérrez Chong, 193–234. Mexico City: Universidad Nacional Autónoma de Mexico.

Blackwell, Maylei. 2006. "Weaving in the Spaces: Transnational Indigenous Women's Organizing and the Politics of Scale." In *Dissident Women: Gender and Cultural Politics in Chiapas*, edited by Shannon Speed, R. Aída Hernández, and Lynn Stephen, 240–318. Austin: University of Texas Press.

Bonfil Batalla, Guillermo. 1996. *Mexico Profundo: Reclaiming a Civilization*, translated by Philip A. Dennis. Austin: University of Texas Press.

Bourdieu, Pierre. 1998. *Practical Reason: On the Theory of Action*. Stanford, Calif.: Stanford University Press.

Brecher, Jeremy, John Brown Child, and Jill Cutler, eds. 1993. *Global Visions: Beyond the New World Order*. Boston: South End.

Bromley, Daniel W. 1991. *Environment and Economy, Property Rights and Public Policy*. Oxford: Basil Blackwell.

Brown, Wendy. 2015. *Undoing the Demos: Neoliberalism's Stealth Revolution*. Princeton, N.J.: Zone Books.

Brown, Wendy, and Veronica Gago. 2020. *Is There a Neoliberalism from Below? A Conversation Between Veronica Gago and Wendy Brown*. New York: Verso.

Brooks, Ethel. 2007. *Unraveling the Garment Industry: Transnational Organizing and Women's Work*. Minneapolis: University of Minnesota Press.

Buroway, Michael, Joseph A. Blum, Sheba George, Zsuzsa Gille, and Millie Thayer, eds. 2000. *Global Ethnography: Forces, Connections, and Imaginations in a Postmodern World*. Berkeley: University of California Press.

Callahan, Manuel. 2003. "Mexican Border Troubles: Social War, Settler Colonialism and the Production of Frontier Discourses, 1848–1880." PhD diss., University of Texas at Austin.

Camin, Héctor, and Lorenzo Meyer. 1993. *In the Shadow of the Mexican Revolution: Contemporary Mexican History, 1910–1989*. Translated by Luis Fierro. Austin: University of Texas Press.

Carrillo, Jorge, and Redi Gomis. 2004. *Encuesta: aprendizaje tecnológico y escalamiento industrial en las plantas maquiladoras*. Tijuana: El Colegio de la Frontera Norte.

Castañeda, Antonia. 1990. "Gender, Race, and Culture: Spanish-Mexican Women in the Historiography of Frontier California." *Frontiers* 11: 8–20.

Castañeda, Antonia. 2007. *Gender and the Borderlands: A Frontiers Reader*. Lincoln: University of Nebraska Press.

Castells, Manuel. 1996. *The Rise of the Network Society: The Information Age*. London: Wiley-Blackwell.

Chant, Sylvia. 1991. *Women and Survival in Mexican Cities: Perspectives on Gender, Labour Markets and Low-Income Households*. Manchester: Manchester University Press.

Chant, Sylvia. 1994. "Women, Work and Household Survival Strategies in Mexico, 1982–1992: Past Trends, Current Tendencies and Future Research." *Bulletin of Latin American Research* 13: 203–33.

Chávez, Daniel. 1998. "El Barzón: Performing Resistance in Contemporary Mexico." *Arizona Journal of Hispanic Cultural Studies* 2: 87–112.

Chávez, Leo R. 1992. *Shadowed Lives: Undocumented Immigrants in American Society*. Orlando, Fla.: Harcourt Brace Jovanovich College.

Cleaver, Harry. 1987. "The Uses of an Earthquake." *Visa Versa* (December–January): https://la.utexas.edu/users/hcleaver/earthquake.html (accessed April 10, 2021).

Coady, David. 2003. "Alleviating Structural Poverty in Developing Countries: The Approach of PROGRESA in Mexico." Background paper, World Development Report, World Bank,. Washington, D.C.

Cohen, Deborah, and Frazier, Lessie. 2009. *Gender and Sexuality in 1968: Transformative Politics in the Cultural Imagination*. New York: Palgrave Macmillan.

Corcoran-Nantes, Yvonne. 2003. "Female Consciousness or Feminist Consciousness? Women's Consciousness Raising in Community-Based Struggles in Brazil." In *Feminist Theory Reader: Local and Global Perspectives*, edited by Carol McCann and Kim Seung-Kyung, 126–37. New York: Routledge.

Coronado, Irasema. 2006. "Styles, Strategies, and Issues of Women Leaders at the Border." In *Women and Change at the U.S.-Mexico Border: Mobility, Labor, And Activism*, 142–58. Tucson: University of Arizona Press.

Cortes, Fernando, and Rosa Maria Rubalcava. 1994. *Autoexplotación Forzada y Equidad por Empobrecimiento: La Distribucion del Ingreso Familiar en Mexico (1977–1984)*. Mexico City: El Colegio de Mexico.

Coulthard, Glenn Sean. 2014. *Red Skin, White Masks: Rejecting the Colonial Politics of Recognition*. Minneapolis: University of Minnesota Press.

Craig, Anne L. 1990. "Institutional Context and Popular Strategies." In *Popular Movements and Political Change in Mexico*, edited by Joe Foweraker and Ann Craig, 271–84. Boulder, Colo.: Lynne Rienner.

Craske, Nikki. 2005. "Ambiguities and Ambivalences in Making the Nation: Women and Politics in 20th-Century Mexico." *Feminist Review* 79: 116–33.

Cruikshank, Barbara. 1999. *The Will to Empower: Democratic Citizens and Other Subjects*. Ithaca, N.Y.: Cornell University Press.

Cuninghame, Patrick, and Carolina B. Corona. 1998. "A Rainbow at Midnight: Zapatistas and Autonomy." *Capital and Class* 22: 12–22.

Cunningham, Hilary. 2004. "Nations Rebound? Crossing Borders in a Gated Globe." *Identities: Global Studies in Culture and Power* 11: 329–50.

Cumes, Aura Estela. 2012. "Mujeres Indígenas, Patriarcado Y Colonialismo Un Desafía A La Segregación Comprensiva De Las Formas De Dominio." *Anuario Hojas De Warmi* 17: 1–16.

Dalla Costa, Mariarosa, and Selma James. 1972. *The Power of Women*. London: Falling, 1972.

Davalos, Enrique. 2004. "A Diez Años que Empezó el Tratado de Libre Comercio (TLC)." *Boletín Maquilero* 1: 2–10.

Davis, Diane E. 1990. "Social Movements in Mexico's Crisis." *Journal of International Affairs* 43: 343–67.

De la Garza Toledo, Enrique. 2010. "The New Economic Model and Spatial Changes in Labour Relations in Post-NAFTA Mexico." In *Employment and Society: Working Space*, edited by Susan McGrath-Champ, Andrew Herod, Al Rainnie, 325–48. Northampton: Edward Elgar.

De la O, Maria Eugenia. 2006. "El trabajo de las mujeres en la industria maquiladora de Mexico: Balance de cuatro décadas de Estudio." *Revista de Antropología Iberoamericana* 1: 404–27.

Deere, Carmen D., and Magdalena León. 2001. *Empowering Women: Land and Property Rights in Latin America*. Pittsburgh: University of Pittsburgh Press.

Delgado Bernal, D., and C. A. Elenes. 2011. "Chicana Feminist Theorizing: Methodologies, Pedagogies, and Practices." In *Chicano School Failure and Success: Present, Past, and Future*, edited by R. R. Valencia, 99–140. 3rd ed. New York: Routledge.

Delgado-Gaitán, Concha. 1993. "Researching Change and Changing the Researcher." *Harvard UniversityEducational Review* 63: 389–411.

Desfor, Gene, Deborah Barndt, and Barbara Rahder, eds. 2002. *Just Doing It: Popular Collective Action in the Americas*. Montréal: Black Rose.

Diario Oficial de la Federación. 1984. "Declaratoria." Accessed February 12, 2020. http://www.dof.gob.mx/.

Diaz-Barriga, Miguel. 1998. "Beyond the Domestic and the Public: Colonas Participation in Urban Movements in Mexico City." In *Cultures of Politics, Politics of Cultures: Re-Visioning Latin American Social Movements*, edited by Sonia E. Alvarez, Evelina Dagnino, and Arturo Escobar, 252–77. Boulder, Colo.: Westview.

Diaz-Polanco, Hector. 1997. *Indigenous Peoples in Latin America: The Quest for Self-Determination*. Boulder, Colo.: Westview.

Dirlik, Arif. 1996. "The Global in the Local." In *Global/Local: Cultural Reproduction and the Transnational Imaginary*, edited by Rob Wilson and Wimal Dissanayake, 21–45. Durham, N.C.: Duke University Press.

Dolhinow, Rebecca. 2006. "Mexican Women's Activism in New Mexico's Colonias." In *Women and Change at the U.S.-Mexico Border: Mobility,*

Labor and Activism, edited by Doreen J. Mattingly and Ellen R. Hansen, 125–41. Tucson: University of Arizona Press.

Dolhinow, Rebecca. 2010. *A Jumble of Needs: Women's Activism and Neoliberalism in the Colonias of the Southwest*. Minneapolis: University of Minnesota Press.

Domínguez, R. Edmé. 2002. "Continental Transnational Activism and Women Workers' Networks Within NAFTA." *International Feminist Journal of Politics* 4: 216–39.

Drukier, Wendy Ellen. 1995. "Understanding Mobilization: Urban Popular Movements and Mèxico's Lost Decade." PhD diss., Carleton University.

Dunn, Timothy. 1996. *The Militarization of the U.S.-Mexico Border, 1978–1992: Low-Intensity Conflict Doctrine Comes Home*. Austin: University of Texas Center for Mexican American Studies.

Eckstein, Susan, ed. 2001. *Power and Popular Protest: Latin American Social Movements*. 2nd ed. Berkeley: University of California Press.

Edelman, Marc. 2001. "Social Movements: Changing Paradigms and Forms of Politics." *Annual Review of Anthropology* 30: 285–317.

Elenes, C. Alejandra. 2011. *Transforming Borders: Chicana/o Popular Culture and Pedagogy*. Lanham, Md.: Lexington.

Escobar, Arturo. 2001. "Culture Sits in Places: Reflections on Globalism and Subaltern Strategies of Localization." *Political Geography* 20: 139–74.

Esteva, Gustavo. 1984. *La batalla en el Mexico Rural*. Mexico City: Siglo XXI Editores.

Esteva, Gustavo. 2001. "The Meaning and Scope of the Struggle for Autonomy." *Latin American Perspectives* 28: 120–48.

Esteva, Gustavo. 2012. "Hope from the Margins." Wealth of the Commons. Accessed November 3. http://wealthofthecommons.org/essay/hope-margins.

Esteva, Gustavo, and Madhu Prakash. [1998] 1999. *Grassroots Post-Modernism: Remaking the Soil of Cultures*. New York: Zed.

Evans, Sarah M. 2009. *Sons, Daughters, and Patriarchy: Gender and the 1968 Generation*. 2nd ed. Oxford: Oxford University Press.

Falcón, Sylvanna. 2006. "National Security and the Violation of Women: Militarized Border Rape at the US-Mexico Border." In *Color of Violence: The incite! Anthology*, edited by INCITE! Women of Color Against Violence, 119–129. Cambridge, Mass.: South End.

Farmer, Paul, Bruce Nizeye, Sara Stulac, and Salmaan Keshavjee. 2006. "Structural Violence and Clinical Medicine." *PLOS Medicene* 3: 1686–91.

Federici, Silvia. 2004. *Caliban and the Witch*. Brooklyn, N.Y.: Autonomedia.

Federici, Silvia. 2012. *Feminism and the Politics of the Commons*. Amherst, Mass.: Levellers.

Fernández-Kelly, Maria. 1983. "Mexican Border Industrialization, Female Labor Force Participation and Migration." In *Women, Men, and the International Division of Labor*, edited by June Nash and Maria Fernández-Kelly, 205–23. Albany: State University of New York.

Flores, Xochi. 2020. "Rewiring Ourselves and Our Spaces of Presupposed Justice: Building Sites of True Liberation with the Son Jarocho/Fandango Community in Los Angeles." Master's thesis, Pacific Oaks College.

Ferree, Myra M., and Aili M. Tripp, eds. 2006. *Global Feminism: Transnational Women's Activism, Organizing, and Human Rights*. New York: New York University Press.

Forbis, Melissa. 2006. "Autonomy and a Handful of Herbs: Contesting Gender and Ethnic Identities Through Healing." In *Dissident Women: Gender and Cultural Politics in Chiapas*, edited by Shannon Speed, R. Aída Hernández Castillo, and Lynn M. Stephen, 176–202. Austin: University of Texas Press.

Forbis, Melissa. 2015. "After Autonomy: The Zapatistas, Insurgent Indigeneity, and Decolonization." *Settler Colonial Studies* 6, no. 4: 365–84.

Foucault, Michel. 1980. "The Confession of the Flesh" (1977). In *Power/Knowledge: Selected Interviews and Other Writings*, edited by Colin Gordon, 194–228. New York: Pantheon.

Francis, Marquise, and Kamilah Newton. 2020. "19 Black Families Purchase 96 Acres of Land to Create a 'Safe Haven' for Black People." Yahoo! News, September 3, 2020. https://news.yahoo.com/19-black-families -purchased-96-acres-of-land-to-create-a-safe-haven-for-black-people -215152697.html.

Fregoso, Rosa Linda. 2007. "Toward a Planetary Civil Society." In *Women and Migration in the U.S.-Mexico Borderlands: A Reader*, edited by Denise A Segura and Patricia Zavella, 35–66. Durham, N.C.: Duke University Press.

Fregoso, Rosa Linda, and Cynthia Bejarano, eds. 2010. *Terrorizing Women: Feminicide in the Americas*. Durham, N.C.: Duke University Press.

Fukuyama, Francis. 2006. *End of History and the Last Man*. New York: Free Press.

Gago, Veronica. 2017. *Popular Pragmatics and Baroque Economies*. Durham, N.C.: Duke University Press.

Galtung, Johan. 1969. "Violence, Peace and Peace Research." *Journal of Peace Research* 6: 167–91.

Gálvez, Alyshia. 2018. *Eating NAFTA: Trade, Food Policies and the Destruction of Mexico*. Berkeley: University of California Press.

Goett, Jennifer. 2016. *Black Autonomy: Race, Gender, and Afro-Nicaraguan Activism*. Stanford, Calif.: Stanford University Press.

Gomez, Alan E. 2016. *The Revolutionary Imaginations of Greater Mexico: Chicana/o Radicalism, Solidarity Politics and Latin American Social Movements*. Austin: University of Texas Press.

Gonzales, Patrisia. 2003. *The Mud People: Chronicles, Testimonios and Remembrances*. San Jose, Calif.: Chusma House.

Gonzalez, Deena. 1999. *Refusing the Favor: The Spanish-Mexican Women of Santa Fe, 1820–1880*. New York: Oxford University Press.

Gonzalez de la Rocha, Mercedes. 1988. "Economic Crisis, Domestic Reorganization and Women's Work in Guadalajara, Mexico." *Bulletin of Latin American Research* 7: 207–23.

González, Gilbert G., and Raúl Fernandez. 2002. "Empire and the Origins of Twentieth-Century Migration from Mexico to the United States." *Pacific Historical Review* 71, no. 1: 19–57.

Gonzalez, Martha. 2020. *Chican@ Artivistas: Music, Community, and Transborder Tactics in East Los Angeles*. Austin: University of Texas Press.

Gonzalez, Pablo. 2011. "Autonomy Road: The Cultural Politics of Chicano/a Autonomous Organizing in Los Angeles, California." PhD diss., University of Texas at Austin.

González Flores, Roberto. 2008. "Chican@ Artists and Zapatistas Walk Together Asking, Listening, Learning: The Role of Transnational Informal Learning Networks in the Creation of a Better World." PhD diss., University of Southern California.

Gonzalez, Sergio. 2012. *The Femicide Machine*. Translated by Michael Parker-Stainback. Cambridge, Mass.: MIT Press.

Grise, Virginia. 2017. *Your Healing Is Killing Me*. Pittsburg, PA: Plays Inverse.

Grosfoguel, Ramón. 2002. "Colonial Difference, Geopolitics of Knowledge and Global Coloniality in the Modern/Colonial Capitalist World-System." *Review* 25: 203–24.

Grosfoguel, Ramón. 2007. "The Epistemic Decolonial Turn." *Cultural Studies* 21: 211–23.

Grosfoguel, Ramón, and Georas, Chloe S. 2000. "'Coloniality of Power' and Racial Dynamics: Notes Toward a Reinterpretation of Latino Caribbeans In New York City." *Identities* 7, no. 1: 85–125.

Guibernau, Montserrat. 1999. *Nations Without States: Political Communities in a Global Age*. Malden, Mass.: Blackwell/Polity.

Gudynas, Eduardo. 2011. "Buen Vivir: Today's Tomorrow." *Development* 54, no. 4: 441–47.

Haber, Paul. 2006. *Power from Experience: Urban Popular Movements in Late Twentieth-Century Mexico*. University Park: Pennsylvania State University Press.

Hamilton, Sarah. 2002. "Neoliberalism, Gender, and Property Rights in Rural Mexico." *Latin American Research Review* 37: 119–43.

Hancox, Dan. 2013. "Marinaleda: Spain's Communist Model Village." *Guardian*, October 19, 2013. https://www.theguardian.com/world/2013/oct/20/marinaleda-spanish-communist-village-utopia.

Hardt, Michael, and Antonio Negri. 2000. *Empire*. Cambridge, Mass.: Harvard University Press.

Hardy-Fanta, Carol. 1997. "Latina Women and Political Consciousness: La chispa que prende." In *Women Transforming Politics: An Alternative Reader*, edited by Cathy J. Chen, Kathleen B. Jones, and Joan C. Tronto, 223–37. New York: New York University Press.

Hart, John Mason. 2002. *Empire and Revolution: The Americans in Mexico Since the Civil War*. Berkeley: University of California Press.

Harvey, David. 2003. *The New Imperialism*. Oxford: Oxford University Press.

Harvey, David. 2007. *A Brief History of Neoliberalism*. Oxford: Oxford University Press.

Hernandez, Roberto D. 2018. *Coloniality of the U.S.-Mexico Border: Power, Violence, and the Decolonial Imperative*. Tucson: University of Arizona Press.

Herzog, Larry. 1990. *Where North Meets South: Cities, Space and Politics on the U.S.-Mexico Border*. Austin: University of Texas Press.

Heyck, Denis Lynn Daly. 2002. *Surviving Globalization in Three Latin American Communities*. Peterborough: Broadview.

Holloway, John. 2019. *Change the World Without Taking Power: The Meaning of Revolution Today*. London: PLUTO.

Holston, James. 2008. *Insurgent Citizenship: Disjunctions of Democracy and Modernity in Brazil*. Princeton, N.J.: Princeton University Press.

Iglesias-Prieto, Norma. 1997. *Beautiful Flowers of the Maquiladora: Life Histories of Women Workers in Tijuana*. Austin: University of Texas Press.

INCITE! Women of Color Against Violence, eds. 2006 *Color of Violence: The incite! Anthology*. Cambridge, Mass.: South End.

Juris, Jeffrey S. 2007. "Practicing Militant Ethnography with the Movement for Global Resistance in Barcelona." In *Constituent Imagination: Militant Investigations//Collective Theorization*, edited by Stevphen Shukaitis, David Graeber, and Erika Biddle, 164–78. Oakland, Calif.: AK.

Keck, Margaret, and Kathryn Sikkink. 1998. *Activists Beyond Borders: Advocacy Networks in International Politics*. Ithaca, N.Y.: Cornell University Press.

King, Amanda. 2006. "Ten Years with NAFTA: A Review of the Literature and an Analysis of Farmer Responses in Sonora and Veracruz, Mexico." Special Report 06–01, CIMMYT/Congressional Hunger Center, Washington, D.C.

Kopinak, Kathryn. 2003. "Globalization in Tijuana Maquiladoras: Using Historical Antecedents and Migration to Test Globalization Models." *Papeles de Población* 9: 219–42.

Kuppers, Gaby, ed. 1994. *Compañeras: Voices from the Latin American Women's Movement*. London: Latin American Bureau.

Laboy, Julio. 1997. "Tijuana Squatters Push Land Battle Across Border." *Wall Street Journal*, February 12, 1997. https://www.wsj.com/articles/SB855686728369280000.

Lara, Orlando. 2003. "Arte, Tierra y dignidad: An Intervention in a Subaltern Community Context." Honors thesis, Stanford University.

Latina Feminist Group. 2001. *Telling to Live: Latina Feminist Testimonios*. Durham, N.C.: Duke University Press.

Laurell, Asa Cristina. 1994. "Pronasol o la pobreza de los programas contra la pobreza." *Nueva Sociedad* 131: 156–70.

Levy, Santiago. 1994. "La pobreza en Mexico." In *La pobreza en Mexico. Causas y políticas para combatirla*, edited by Félix Vélez, 15–112. Mexico City: ITAM y Fondo de Cultura de Economico.

Liebowitz, Debra. 2002. "Gendering (Trans)national Advocacy." *International Feminist Journal of Politics* 4: 173–96.

Lister, Ruth. 2003. *Citizenship: Feminist Perspectives*. New York: New York University Press.

Logan, Kathleen. 1990. "Women's Participation in Urban Protest." In *Popular Movements and Political Change in Mexico*, edited by Joe Foweraker and Ann L. Craig, 150–60. Boulder, Colo.: Lynne Rienner.

Lomas, Clara. 2007. "Transborder Discourse: The Articulation of Gender in the Borderlands in the Early Twentieth Century." In *Gender and the Borderlands: The Frontiers Reader*, edited by Antonia Castaneda, 51–74. Lincoln: University of Nebraska Press.

Lorey, David. 1999. *The U.S.-Mexico Border in the Twentieth Century: A History of Economic and Social Transformation*. Wilmington, Del.: Scholarly Resources.

Lugones, Maria. 2007. "Heterosexualism and the Colonial/Modern Gender System." *Hypatia* 22: 186–209.

Lugo, Alejandro. 2000. "Destabilizing the Masculine, Refocusing 'Gender': Men and the Aura of Authority in Michelle Z. Rosaldo's Work." In *Gender Matters: Rereading Michelle Z. Rosaldo*, edited by Alejandro Lugo and Bill Maurer, 54–89. Ann Arbor: University of Michigan Press.

Magaña, Maurice Rafael. 2020. *Cartographies of Youth Resistance: Hip-Hop, Punk, and Urban Autonomy in Mexico*. Oakland: University of California Press.

Mahmood, Saba. 2005. *Politics of Piety: The Islamic Revival and the Feminist Subject*. Princeton, N.J.: Princeton University Press.

Mancillas, Manuel. 2001. "Mistaken Identities." *Variant* 12: https://romulusstudio.com/variant/12texts/Mancillas.html (accessed April 9, 2021).

Mancillas, Manuel. 2002. "Transborder Collaboration: the Dynamics of Grassroots Globalization." In *Globalization on the Line: Culture, Capital, and Citizenship at U.S. Borders*, edited by Claudia Sadowski-Smith, 201–20. New York: Palgrave Macmillan.

Maquiladoras: Explotación y Resistencia. 2010. "Maquiladoras 101." Accessed February 12, 2020. http://sdmaquila.blogspot.com/2010/02/maquiladoras-101-english.html#more.

Marchand, Marianne H., and Anne Glisson Runyan, eds. 2011. *Gender and Global Restructuring: Sightings, Sites, and Resistances*. 2nd ed. New York: Routledge.

Mares, Teresa, and Devon G. Peña. 2010. "Urban Agriculture in the Making of Insurgent Spaces in Los Angeles and Seattle." In *Insurgent Public Space: Guerrilla Urbanism and the Remaking of Public Space*, edited by Jeffrey Hou, 241–54. New York: Routledge.

Mares, Teresa, and Devon G. Peña. 2011. "Environmental and Food Justice: Toward Local, Slow, and Deep Food Systems." In *Cultivating Food Justice: Race, Class, and Sustainability*, edited by Alison Alkon and Julian Agyeman, 197–219. Cambridge, Mass.: MIT Press.

Martinez, Oscar. 1988. *Troublesome Border*. Tucson: University of Arizona Press.

Martínez, Oscar. 1994. *Border People: Life and Society in the U.S.-Mexico Borderlands*. Tucson: University of Arizona Press.

Martinez, Theresa A. 1996. "Toward a Chicana Feminist Epistemological Standpoint: Theory at the Intersection of Race, Class, and Gender." *Race, Gender, and Class* 3: 107–28.

Martinez Luna, Jaime. 2015. "Comunalidad as the Axis of Oaxacan Thought in Mexico." Upside Down World, October 27, 2015. http://upsidedownworld.org/archives/mexico/comunalidad-axis-of-oaxacan-thought/.

Mattiace, Shannan L. 2002. "Una Nueva Idea de Nación: Autonomía Indígena en Mexico." In *Tierra, Libertad y Autonomía: Impactos Regionales del Zapatismo en Chiapas*, edited by Shannan L. Mattiace, Rosalva Aída Hernándes and Jan Rus, 229–68. Mexico City: Centro de Investigaciones y Estudios Superiores en Antropologia Social.

Meinzen-Dick, Ruth, Lynn Brown, Hilary Feldstein, and Agnes Quisumberg. 1997. "Gender, Property Rights, and Natural Resources." *World Development* 25: 1303–15.

Melucci, Alberto. 1989. *Nomads of the Present: Social Movements and Individual Needs in Contemporary Society*. London: Hutchenson Radius.

Mendez, Alfredo. 2012. "Mujeres y hombres de la maquila: bajos sueldos y se pagan su propio seguro social." La Jornada, September 24, 2012. http://www.jornada.unam.mx/ultimas/.

Menjivar, Cecilia 2011. *Enduring Violence: Ladina Women's Lives in Guatemala*. Berkeley: University of California Press.

Mies, Maria. 1998. *Patriarchy and Accumulation on a World Scale: Women in the International Division of Labour*. London: Zed.

Mignolo, Walter D. 2000. *Local Histories/Global Designs*. Princeton, N.J.: Princeton University Press.

Mignolo, Walter D. 2007. "Delinking: The Rhetoric of Modernity, The Logic of Coloniality, and the Grammar of De-Coloniality." *Cultural Studies* 21: 449–514.

Miranda, J., 2016. "Inegi: sólo 2 de cada 10 mujeres del campo poseen tierras." La Jornada. Accessed March 31, 2021. https://www.jornada.com.mx/2016/11/11/estados/028n1eco.

Mirande, Alfredo. 1987. *Gringo Justice*. Notre Dame, Ind.: University of Notre Dame Press.

Miyoshi, Masao. 1996. "A Borderless World? From Colonialism to Transnationalism and the Decline of the Nation State." In *Global/Local: Cultural Reproduction and the Transnational Imaginary*. Durham, N.C.: Duke University Press.

Moghadam, Valentine M. 2001. "Transnational Feminist Networks: Collective Action in an Era of Globalization." In *Globalization and Social Movements*, edited by Pierre Hamel, Henri Lustiger-Thaler, Jan Nederveen Peiterse and Sasha Poseneil, 111–33. New York: Palgrave Macmillan.

Mohanty, Chandra Talpade. 2003. *Feminism Without Borders: Decolonizing Theory, Practicing Solidarity*. Durham, N.C.: Duke University Press.

Mora, Mariana. 2003. "The Imagination to Listen: Reflections on a Decade of Zapatista Struggle." *Social Justice/Global Options* 30, no. 3: 17–31.

Mora, Mariana. 2008. "Decolonizing Politics: Zapatista Indigenous Autonomy in an Era of Neoliberal Governance and Low Intensity Warfare." PhD diss., University of Texas at Austin.

Mora, Mariana. 2017. *Kuxlejal Politics: Indigenous Autonomy, Race and Decolonizing Research in Zapatista Communities*. Austin: University of Texas Press.

Morales, Maria Cristina, and Cynthia Bejarano. 2009. "Transnational Sexual and Gendered Violence: An Application of Border Sexual Conquest at a Mexico–U.S. Border." *Global Networks* 9: 420–39.

Moyao, Eliseo M. 1991. "Hay un cambio de fondo en la politica social del gobierno?" *Barrio Nuevo: Andlisis Urbano* 1: 1–5.

Nash, June C. 2001. *Mayan Visions: The Quest for Autonomy in an Age of Globalization*. New York: Routledge.

Nevins, Joseph. 2002. *Operation Gatekeeper: The Rise of the "Illegal Alien" and the Making of the U.S.-Mexico Boundary*. New York: Routledge.

Niño-Zarazúa, Miguel. 2010. *Mexico's Progresa-Oportunidades and the Emergence of Social Assistance in Latin America*. Brooks World Poverty Institute, University of Manchester.

Nunez, Guillermina Gina, and Georg M. Klamminger. 2010. "Centering the Margins: The Transformation of Community in Colonias on the U.S.-Mexico border." In *Cities and Citizenship at the U.S.-Mexico Border: The Paso (del Norte)*, edited by Kathleen Staudt, Cesar M. Fuentes, and Julia E Monárrez Fragoso, 147–72. New York: Palgrave Macmillan.

Olivera, Mercedes. 2010. "Violencia Feminicida: Violence Against Women and Mexico's Structural Crisis." In *Terrorizing Women: Feminicide in the Americas*, edited by Rosa-Linda Fregoso and Cynthia Bejarano, 49–59. Durham, N.C.: Duke University Press.

Ortiz, Desiree. 2012. "Las maquilas y la explotación de la mujer Mexicana." Paper, Universidad Pedagógica Experimental Libertador, Maturín, July 2012. http://www.monografias.com/trabajos93/maquilas-y-explotacion

-mujer-mexicana/maquilas-y-explotacion-mujer-mexicana2.shtml (accessed February 12, 2020).

Ortiz, Tereza. 2001. *Never Again a World Without Us: Voices of Mayan Women in Chiapas, Mexico*. Washington, D.C.: EPICA.

Ortiz-Gonzalez, Victor. 2004. *El Paso: Local Frontiers at a Global Crossroads*. Minneapolis: University of Minnesota Press.

Ovalle, Lilian Paola, Alfonso Díaz Tovar, and Luis Arturo Ongay. 2014. "Pensar la memoria desde la frontera: recuerdo, reconstrucción y reconciliación en el caso del 'pozolero.'" *A Contracorriente: A Journal on Social History and Literature in Latin America* 12, no. 1: 278–300.

Pardo, Mary. 1998. *Mexican American Women Activists: Identity and Resistance in Two Los Angeles Communities*. Philadelphia: Temple University Press.

Paredes, Julieta. 2013. *Hilando Fino: Desde el feminismo comunitario*. Mexico City: Cooperativa El Rebozo.

Parenti, Christian. 1999. *Lockdown America: Police and Prisons in the Age of Crisis*. London: Verso.

Pastor, Manuel, and Carol Wise. 1994. "The Origins and Sustainability of Mexico's Free Trade Policy." *International Organization* 48: 459–89.

Peña, Devon. 1997. *Terror of the Machine: Technology, Work, Gender, and Ecology of the U.S.-Mexico Border*. Austin: University of Texas.

Peña, Devon. 2005. "Autonomy, Equity and Environmental Justice." In *Power, Justice and the Environment: A Critical Appraisal of the Environmental Justice Movement*, edited by David Naguib Pellow and Robert J. Brulle, 131–52. Cambridge, Mass.: MIT Press.

Peña, Milagros. 2007. *Latina Activists Across Borders: Women Grassroots Organizing in Mexico and Texas*. Durham, N.C.: Duke University Press.

Pezzoli, Keith. 1987. "The Urban Land Problem and Popular Sector Housing Development in Mexico City." *Environment and Behavior* 19: 371–97.

Pleyers, Geoffrey. 2011. *Alter-Globalization: Becoming Actors in a Global Age*. Malden, Mass.: Polity.

Pool, Emilia. 2008. "Tijuana's Maquiladoras: Producing Resistance." *Rebeldia* 5: 25–35.

Povinelli, Elizabeth A. 2013. *Economies of Abandonment: Social Belonging and Endurance in Late Liberalism*. Durham, N.C.: Duke University Press.

Quijano, Aníbal. 1993. "Raza, Etnia y Nación En Mariátegui: Cuestiones Abiertas." In *José Carlos Mariátegui y Europa: El Otro Aspecto del Descubrimiento*, 167–87. Lima: Empresa Editoria Amauta S.A.

Quijano, Aníbal. 1998. "La Colonialidad del Poder y la Experiencia Cultural Latinoamericana." In *Pueblo, Epóca y Desarrollo: La Sociología de América Latina*, 139–55. Caracas: Nueva Sociedad.

Quijano, Aníbal. 2000. "A Coloniality of Power, Eurocentrism and Latin America." *Nepantla: Views From the South* 1: 533–80.

Ramirez, Jorge. "Becoming Indigenous: Race, Violence, and Indigeneity between Southern Mexico and the U.S.-Mexican Pacific Coast, 1970-1994." PhD diss., University of California, San Diego.

Randall, Margaret. 1995. *Our Voices, Our Lives: Stories of Women from Central America and the Caribbean*. Monroe, Maine: Common Courage.

Rentería Pedraza, Víctor Hugo, and Andrea Spears Kirkland. 2008. "Migracion y trabajo en la frontera norte." Paper, Third International Sociology Congress, "Imagining Sociology of the 21st Century," Universidad Autonoma de Baja California, Ensenada, Mexico.

Roberts, Jorge S. 2001. "The Reasons for Mexico's Trade Liberalization." University of Washington. Accessed March 31, 2021. https://citeseerx.ist.psu.edu/viewdoc/download?doi=10.1.1.196.7265&rep=rep1&type=pdf.

Roman, Leslie, and Michael Apple. 1990. "Is Naturalism a Move Away from Positivism? Materialist and Feminist Approaches to Subjectivity in Ethnographic Research." In *Qualitative Inquiry in Education: The Continuing Debate*, edited by Elliot Eisner and Alan Peshkin, 38–73. New York: Teachers College.

Rosaldo, Renato. 1989. *Culture and Truth: The Remaking of Social Analysis*. Boston: Beacon.

Rubio-Goldsmith, Raquel, Celestino Fernández, Jessie K. Finch, and Araceli Masterson-Algar, eds. 2016. *Migrant Deaths in the Arizona Desert: La vida no vale nada*. Tucson: University of Arizona Press.

Russel y Rodríguez, Mónica. 1998. "Confronting Anthropology's Silencing Praxis: Speaking Of/From a Chicana Consciousness." *Qualitative Inquiry* 4: 15–40.

Russel y Rodríguez, Mónica. 2000. "Mexicanas and Mongrels: Policies of Hybridity, Gender and Nation in the U.S.-Mexican War." *Latino Studies Journal* 11: 49–73.

Rycenga, Jennifer, and Marguerite Waller. 2000. *Frontline Feminisms: Women, War, and Resistance*. New York: Garland.

Sadowski-Smith, Claudia. 2002. "Border Studies, Diaspora, and Theories of Globalization." In *Globalization on the Line: Culture, Capital, and*

Citizenship at U.S. Borders, edited by Claudia Sadowski-Smith, 1–27. New York: Palgrave Macmillan.

Safa, Helen I. 1990. "Women's Social Movements in Latin America." *Gender & Society* 4: 354–69.

Safran, William. 2000. "Spatial and Functional Dimensions of Autonomy: Cross-National and Theoretical Perspectives." In *Identity and Territorial Autonomy in Plural Societies*, edited by Willian Safran and Ramon Maiz, 11–34. Portland, Maine: Frank Cass.

Said, Edward. 1978. *Orientalism: Western Representations of the Orient*. London: Routledge/Kegan Paul.

Sainz, Pablo. 2008. "Maclovio Rojas: 20 Years of Struggle for Dignity." La Prensa San Diego. Accessed March 31, 2021. http://laprensa-sandiego .org/archieve/2008/april18-08/Maclovio.htm.

Sandoval, Chela. 2000. *Methodology of the Oppressed*. Minneapolis: University of Minnesota Press.

Sassen, Saskia. 1998. *Globalization and its Discontents*. New York: New Press.

Sassen, Saskia. 2003. "The Participation of States and Citizens in Global Governance." *Indiana Journal of Global Legal Studies* 10: 5–28.

Sassen, Saskia. 2005. "The Repositioning of Citizenship and Alienage: Emergent Subjects and Spaces for Politics." *Globalizations* 2: 79–94.

Schmidt Camacho, Alicia R. 2005. "The Repositioning of Citizenship and Alienage: Emergent Subjects and Spaces for Politics." *Globalizations* 2: 79–94.

Schmidt Camacho, Alicia R. 2008. *Migrant Imaginaries: Latino Cultural Politics in the U.S.-Mexico Borderlands*. New York: New York University Press.

Segato, Rita Laura. 2014. *Las nuevas formas de la guerra y el cuerpo de las mujeres*. Puebla: Pez en el árbol, 2014.

Segura, Denise A., and Patricia Zavella. 2007. *Women and Migration in the U.S.-Mexico Borderlands: A Reader*. Durham, N.C.: Duke University Press.

Shiva, Vandana. 1988. *Staying Alive: Women, Ecology, and Development*. London: Zed.

Simmons, William, Cecilia Menjívar, and Michelle Téllez. 2015. "Violence and Vulnerability of Migrants in Drop Houses in Arizona." *Violence Against Women* 21, no. 5: 551–70.

Simmons, William, and Michelle Téllez. Forthcoming. "Sexual Violence Against Migrant Women and Children." In *Localizing Human Rights Abuses: The U.S.-Mexico Experience*, edited by William Simmons, Julie Murphy-Erfani, and Carol Mueller.

Sitrin, Marina. 2012. *Everyday Revolutions: Horizontalism And Autonomy in Argentina*. London: Zed.

Sitrin, Marina. 2014. "Definitions of Horizontalism and Autonomy." *NACLA Report on the Americas* 47, no. 3: https://nacla.org/article/definitions-horizontalism-and-autonomy (accessed April 20, 2021).

Sklair, Leslie. 1989. *Assembling for Development: The Maquiladora Industry in Mexico and the United States*. Boston: Unwin Hyman.

Skoufias, Emmanuel, Susan Parker, Jere Behrman, and Carola Pessino. 2001. "Conditional Cash Transfers and Their Impact on Child Work and Schooling: Evidence from the PROGRESA Program in Mexico." *Economía* 2: 45–96.

Smith, Andrea. 2005. "Looking to the Future: Domestic Violence, Women of Color, the State, and Social Change." In *Domestic Violence at the Margins: Readings on Race, Class, Gender and Culture*, edited by Natalie J. Sokoloff, 416–34. New Brunswick, N.J.: Rutgers University Press.

Smith, Andrea. 2008. "American Studies Without America: Native Feminisms and the Nation-State." *American Quarterly* 60: 309–315.

Smith, Michael P., and Luis E. Guarnizo. 1998. *Transnationalism from Below*. New Brunswick, N.J.: Transaction.

Smith, Robert C. 2003. "Migrant Membership as an Instituted Process: Transnationalization, the State, and the Extra-Territorial Conduct of Mexican Politics." *International Migration Review* 37: 297–343.

Soden, Dennis L. 2006. "At the Cross Roads: U.S.-Mexico Border Counties in Transition." Paper 27, IPED Technical Reports. Paper 27. Accessed April 16, 2021. http://digitalcommons.utep.edu/iped_techrep/27.

Speed, Shannon, R. Aída Hernández, and Lynn Stephen, eds. 2006. *Dissident Women: Gender and Cultural Politics in Chiapas*. Austin: University of Texas Press.

Stahler-Sholk, Richard. 2008. "Resisting Neoliberal Homogenization: The Zapatista Autonomy Movement." In *Latin American Social Movements in the Twenty-First Century: Resistance, Power, and Democracy*, edited by Richard Stahler-Sholk, Harry E. Vanden, and Glen David Kuecker, 113–29. Lanham, Md.: Rowman & Littlefield.

Stahler-Sholk, Richard. 2017. "Constructing Autonomy: Zapatista Strategies Indigenous Resistance in Mexico." In *The New Global Politics: Global Social Movements in the Twenty-First Century*, 13–28. London: Routledge.

Starr, Amory, and Jason Adams. 2003. "Anti-Globalization: The Global Fight for Local Autonomy." *New Political Science* 25: 19–42.

Staudt, Kathleen, and Irasema Coronado. 2002. *Fronteras no Mas: Toward Social Justice at the U.S.-Mexico Border*. New York: Palgrave Macmillan.

Stavenhagen, Rodolfo. 1999. "Prólogo." In *Experiencias de Autonomía Indígena*, edited by Aracely Burguete Cal and Mayor, 1–12. Copenhagen: IWGIA.

Stephen, Lynn. 1992. "Women in Mexico's Popular Movements: Survival Strategies against Ecological and Economic Impoverishment." *Latin American Perspectives/The Ecological Crisis of Latin America* 19: 73–96.

Stephen, Lynn. [1997] 2003. *Women and Social Movements in Latin America: Power from Below*. Austin: University of Texas Press.

Stone-Mediatore, Shari. 2003. *Reading Across Borders: Storytelling and Knowledges of Resistance*. New York: Palgrave Macmillan.

Talcott, Molly. 2014. "'Together We Have Power': Personal Traumas and Political Responses Among Activist Oaxaqueñas." *Latin American Perspectives* 41, no. 1: 72–88.

"Tanya Aguiñiga on the History of Maclovio Rojas." Craft in America. Accessed March 31, 2021. https://www.craftinamerica.org/short/tanya-aguiniga-on-the-history-of-maclovio-rojas-mexico.

Telesurtv. 2019. "Land Rights Still Elusive for Women in Mexico." March 3, 2019. https://www.telesurenglish.net/news/Land-Rights-Still-Ellusive-For-Women-In-Mexico-20190303-0009.html.

Téllez, Michelle. 2005. "Doing Research at the Borderlands: Notes from a Chicana Feminist Ethnographer." *Chicana/Latina Studies: Journal of Mujeres Activas en Letras y Cambio Social* 4: 46–70.

Téllez, Michelle. 2008. "Community of Struggle: Gender, Violence, and Resistance on the U.S./Mexico Border." *Gender & Society* 22: 545–67.

Téllez, Michelle. 2013. "Transfronteriza: Gender Rights at the Border and 'La Colectiva Feminista.'" In *Immigrant Women Workers in the Neoliberal Age*, edited by Anna Guevarra, Grace Chang, Maura Toro-Morn, and Nilda Flores, 232–46. Champaign: University of Illinois Press.

Téllez, Michelle, William Simmons, and Mariana del Hierro. 2018. "Border Crossings and Sexual Conquest in the Age of Neoliberalism in the Sonoran Desert." *International Feminist Journal of Politics* 20, no. 4: 524–41.

Thayer, Millie. 2010. *Making Transnational Feminism: Rural Women, NGO Activists, and Northern Donors in Brazil*. New York: Routledge.

Tiano, Susan. 1987. "Women's Work and Unemployment in Northern Mexico." In *Women on the U.S.-Mexico Border: Responses to Change*, edited by Vicki Ruiz and Susan Tiano, 77–102. Winchester: Allen & Unwin.

Tomlinson, Barbara, and Lipsitz, George. 2019. *Insubordinate Spaces: Improvisation and Accompaniment for Social Justice*. Philadelphia: Temple University Press.

Tornell, Aaron. 1995. "Are Economic Crises Necessary for Trade Liberalization and Fiscal Reform? The Mexican Experience." In *Reform, Recovery, and Growth: Latin America and the Middle East*, edited by Rudiger Dornbusch and Sebastien Edwards, 53–76. Chicago: University of Chicago Press.

Trinidad Galvan, Ruth. 2005. "Transnational Communities En La Lucha: Campesinas and Grassroots Organizations Globalization from Below." *Journal of Latinos and Education* 4: 3–20.

Trinidad Galvan, Ruth. 2008. "Global Restructuring, Transmigration, and Mexican Rural Women Who Stay Behind: Accommodating, Contesting, and Transcending Ideologies." *Globalizations* 5: 523–40.

Valenzuela-Arce, Jose M. 1991. *Empapados de Sereno: El Movimiento Urbano Popular en Baja California (1928–1988)*. Tijuana: El Colegio de la Frontera Norte.

Valencia Triana, Margarita (Sayak). 2018. *Gore Capitalism*. Translated by John Pluecker. South Pasadena, Calif.: Semiotext(e).

Villenas, Sofía. 1996a. "Una Buena Educación: Women Performing Life Histories of Moral Education in New Latino Communities." PhD diss., University of North Carolina, Chapel Hill.

Villenas, Sofía.1996b. "The Colonizer/Colonized Chicana Ethnographer: Identity, Marginalization, and Co-optation in the Field." *Harvard Educational Review* 66, no. 4: 711–32.

Wallerstein, Immanuel Maurice. 1991. *Geopolitics and Geoculture*. Cambridge: Cambridge University Press.

Watson, Iain. 2002. *Rethinking the Politics of Globalization: Theory, Concepts and Strategy*. Hampshire: Ashgate.

Weisbrot, Mark, Lara Merling, Vitor Mello, Stephan Lefebvre, and Joseph Sammut. 2018. "Did NAFTA Help Mexico? An Update After 23 Years." *Mexican Law Review* 1, no. 1: 159–83.

Wilson Gilmore, Ruth. 2007. *Golden Gulag: Prisons, Surplus, Crisis, and Opposition in Globalizing California*. Berkeley: University of California Press.

Wolford, Wendy. 2004. "This Land Is Ours: Spatial Imaginaries and the Struggle for Land in Brazil." *Annals of the Association of American Geographers* 94: 409–24.

Yaschine, Iliana. 1999. "The Changing Anti-Poverty Agenda: What Can the Mexican Case Tell Us?" *IDS Bulletin* 30: 47–60.

Zavella, Patricia. 1993. "Feminist Insider Dilemmas: Constructing Ethnic Identity with Chicana Informants." *Frontiers* 13, no. 3: 53–76.

Zibechi, Raul. 2012. *Territories in Resistance: A Cartography of Latin American Social Movements*. Oakland, Calif.: AK.

Zugman, Kara Ann. 2005. "Zapatismo and Urban Political Practice." *Latin American Perspectives* 32, no. 4: 133–47.

Zulaica, Pablo. 2015. "La Lucha Por Existir De Un Barrio Fronterizo." El País, July 15, 2015. https://elpais.com/elpais/2015/07/10/planeta_futuro/1436523467_965848.html.

Index

Los Able Minded Poets, 135
Abu-Lughod, Lila, 74
Agrarian Reform Department,
  47–48
Aguascalientes Community Center,
  50, 68, 74, 102–103, 135, 137–38;
  closure, 156; founding of, 162n5;
  photographs of, 5, 30, 141; sign at
  entrance, 118
Ahora Madrid, 4, 146
Alianza Para el Campo, 43
Alma, 50; critique of the government, 82
amparo, 81
anarchist, 62
asamblea, 4, 58, 68, 74, 155n2
autonomía, 19, 30, 100; academia
  and, 157n1; activism and, 73–74;
  anti-globalization, 98; and the
  body, 104; local, 104; in Maclovio
  Rojas, 57, 121, 130; Magaña's
  ethnography in Oaxaca, 163n2
Aztlan Media Collective, 138

Baja California: Article 226, 81;
  Colectiva Feminista Binacional
  encuentro, 139; development of
  region, 53–54, 62; disputed lands,
  27, 50; elections against PRI, 50,
  71–72; Puertos al Futuro, 80. *See
  also* Ernesto Ruffo-Appel
banking institutions, 99–100
Barros Nock, Magdalena, 51
El Barzón, 99
Bechtel Corporation, 99
Bennett, Vivienne, 64
Bickham Mendez, Jennifer, 9, 19,
  22–23
Blackwell, Maylei, 76, 104
Bolivia: social movements, 61, 141
Bonfil Batalla, Guillermo, and Philip
  Dennis, 32; *Mexico profundo*, 32,
  119
Border Arts Workshop/Taller de
  Arte Fronterizo (BAW/TAF), 72,
  134–35, 138, 163n1; photographs
  of, 135, 137

Border Industrialization Program (BIP), 54
Bracero Program, 54

Calderón, President Felipe, 140, 149
Cárdenas, President Lázaro, 35, 39
cargos (mutual responsibility), 19
Casa de la Mujer, 6, 11, 58, 91, 111–14; "Coatlicue" statue, 91, 93; context of separations and safe spaces, 91, 94; costs, 111; photographs of, 92–93
Castañeda, Antonia, 22, 46
Centro Cultural de Tijuana (CECUT), 140, 159n13
Chiapas, Mexico: Zapatista and, 102–103
child care, 37, 58, 68, 91, 111–14. See also Case de la Mujer; maquilas
Clandestine Workers Party (Union of the People-Party of the Poor, or PROCUP-PDLP), 63
Cleaver, Harry, 66
Central Independiente de Obreros Agrígolas y Campesinos (CIOAC), 64, 159n1
Cochabamba Declaration, 99
Colective Feminista Binacional, 139; encuentro, 139–40
collective identity, 9, 25, 128, 130; transfronteriza cross-border, 139, 157n15
collective resistance, 11, 24, 75, 84
colonias, 17–18, 73, 84
community citizenship, 23, 105, 115, 119, 124, 126; buen vivir, 158n10; maternal dimension of, 119–20, 132
Confederation of Mexican Workers (CMT), 38
Constitution of 1917, 14, 35, 143; Article 27, 39, 47, 104; right of women, 116

coordinadoras, 63
La Coordinadora Nacional del Movimiento Urbano Popular (National Coordination of Urban Populaar Movements, or CONAMUP), 63, 65
La Coordinadora Nacional Plan de Ayala (National Coordination Plan Ayala, or CNPA), 63, 65
La Coordinadora Nacional de Trabajadores de la Educación (National Coordination of Education Workers, or CNTE), 63, 65
La Coordinadora Única de Damnificados (Only Committee of Victims, or CUD), 65
Cruikshank, Barbara, 73
cultural centers (centros sociales), 4

de la Madrid, President Miguel, 36–9
Diaz-Barriga, Miguel, 78; necesidad, 105; private and public spheres, 96–97, 133
Diaz-Polanco, Hector, 32, 102
Dirlik, Arif, 57
Dolhinow, Rebecca, 18, 73, 78, 84, 133, 143; see also colonias
domestic violence, 77
Dora, 9, 21, 58, 60; at asamblea in Aguascalientes, 74–75; centrality of water, 124; community citizenship, 119; critique of the neoliberal state, 123; perspective on leadership, 67, 100–101, 114; on schooling and community work, 110; toll of activism, 142

ejido, 15, 39–40, 47–51; land evasion, 64

Elenes, Alejandra, 18
esperanza, 141, 152
Esteva, Gustavo, 157n1; and Madhu Prakash, 99
ethnography, 7, 11, 16, 20; militant, 21; as participant observer, 7, 77, 159n12; use of pseudonyms, 157n14

Federici, Silvia, 158n7, 161n9
Flores, Xochi, 156n7
Flores Magon, Ricardo and Enrique, 62
food sovereignty, 99, 112
Forbis, Melissa, 75, 122, 147
foreign debt, 36
Foucault, Michel, 17
Fregoso, Rosa Linda, and Cynthia Bejarano, 46
La Frente Nacional por la Libertad y los Derechos de las Mujeres (The National Front Women's Rights and Liberty, or FNALIDM), 64
la frontera, 23, 47

Gago, Veronica, 99, 145
Galtung, Johan, 17
García, Rubén, 6
gender: citizenship and nationalism, 27, 115–16; culturally defined expectations, 23, 25, 41, 163n3; feminization of poverty, 18, 116, 131, 133, 145; and structural violence, 13, 24, 46, 57, 96; subjectivity and resistance, 29–30, 59, 61, 76, 84, 99
Global South, 10, 16, 31, 73
golpe, 81–82
Gomez, Alan, definition of solidarity, 134
Gonzalez, Martha: on hope and possibility, 140, 156n7

Gonzalez, Pablo: analysis of the commons, 115, 156n7
Grosfoguel, Ramón, 32–33

Hardt, Michael, and Antonio Negri, 30
Hardy-Fanta, Carol, 11
Holloway, John, 132, 146
Holston, James, 117
hope. *See esperanza*
Hernández, President Hortensia. 9, 29, 33–34, 62; on building Aguascalientes, 102; critiques of *maquilas*, 79; EZLN comparison, 103; incarceration of, 128–29, 162n9; leadership of, 67–68, 82, 88, 128, 149, 162n4; mural of, 136; photograph of, 30, 145; toll of activism, 142; women-centered political subjectivity, 107–109, 141, 143–45
Huato, Elizabeth, 86, 105–107; on community citizenship, 120, 137–38; mural by, 136; photograph of, 137
Hyundai Corporation, 33–34, 52, 76, 79, 103; battle over land with Maclovio Rojas, 138, 160n4

Institutional Revolutionary Party (PRI), 38; independent organizations, 66, 160n5
International Monetary Fund (IMF), 42, 44
interviews, 7–8

jefas de manzana, 67
Juana, 9, 21; critique of the State, 90; political consciousness, 90–91; self-determination, 91, 117

King, Amanda, 43

latifundismo, 47

Lázaro Cárdenas Ejido Union (Land Union of Lazaro Cardenas, or ULEC), 63

Liga 23 de Septiembre, 63

Lister, Ruth, 117; political citizenship, 124

Lugo, Alejandro, 22

Luz, 9, 80, 105–107; on the importance of unity, 127, 129–30

Maclovianas: activism, 23, 144–45; collective goals, 100, 117, 122, 128; emergent political subjectivity, 60, 77–78, 90–91, 107, 121; horizontalism and, 68, 115; and the neoliberal state, 24, 76, 104, 118, 133; all-night vigil, 50

Maclovio Rojas: *El Boletin Zapata*, 102; Cerro de Esperanza, 48; Colective Feminista Binacional, 139; corrido in honor of, 160n2; counterhegemony, 133; *Everyone Their Grain of Sand*, 140; founding, 28, 79; geographic location, 28; maquiladoras, 52; mural of, 29; parallels with Zapatistas, 102, 120; political citizenship, 124, 143; support for, 134, 138; toll of activism on women, 142; women-centered spaces, 138–39. *See also* autonomía

Mancillas, Manuel, 72, 163n1

maquila, 43, 49–50, 52, 55–56, 68; and the environment, 83, 125; gender and women workers, 56, 108, 111, 129, 131, 139; *transfronteriza* cross-border solidarity, 157n15

La Marcha por la Libertad, 72, 128

Doña Maria, 9, 21; on a borderlands subjectivity, 87–89, 122; proposal

for new school, 76; and research 77–78; toll of activism, 142

Martinez, John, 138

Martínez, Oscar: borderlands, 158n6

Martínez Luna, Jaime: on *comunalidad*, 101–102

mestizaje, 32, 160n6, 162n3

Mexican Revolution, 29, 35, 47, 116, 143

militarization, 42, 45

Mohanty, Chandra Tapalde, 10

Mora, Mariana, 14

Morales, Maria Cristina, and Cynthia Bejarano, 17, 47

mujeres fronterizas, 14, 20, 23, 25, 96, 132–33, 145

National Agrarian Registry (RAN), 40

National Confederation of Popular Organizations (CNOP), 38

National Coordinating Bodies, 63; *see also* coordinadoras

National Peasant Confederation (CNC), 38

necesidad, 100, 105; influence on Maclovianas, 110, 113; and neoliberal neglect, 107; as source of creative tension, 115

neoliberal neglect, 19, 30, 35, 60; agency and political subjectivity, 98, 105, 130, 133; critiques by Maclovianas, 123; and *necesidad*, 107

neoliberal privatization policies, 17, 19, 38–39, 42, 51, 99; systems of gendered power, 131. *See also* maquilas

neoliberalism: gender and, 145; ideology of, 14–15; policies, 17–19, 47; and social movements,

46, 98–100, 119, 142. *See also* autonomía, community citizenship

Nicolasa: at *asamblea* in Aguascalientes, 74–75; incarceration of, 81, 163n7; leadership of, 149

nongovernmental organization (NGO): and the neoliberal state, 18, 73, 84, 143; women's activism, 94

North American Free Trade Agreement (NAFTA): background, 39–42; and accelerated rate of globalization practices, 51, 54–56, 131; and Mexican migrants, 45; threat to Indigenous peoples, 42–43, 55

North Dakota: social movements, 141

Okupas, 4, 155n1
Olivera, Mercedes, 40
Operation Gatekeeper, 45
Ortiz, Tereza, 57
Ortiz-Gonzalez, 22, 45, 53
Osuna, Artemio, 163n6; mural of, 136

PAN, 71
Pardo, Mary: political participation, 97
Paredes, Julieta, 61
El Partido Liberal Mexicano (The Mexican Liberal Party), 62
Partido de los Pobres (Party of the Poor, of PP), 63
Partido Revolucionario Obrero Clandestino-Union del Pueblo (Revolutionary Workers Clandestine Union of the People, or PROCUP), 63
Pastor, Manuel, and Carol Wise, 37

Paula, 9, 50; oppositional consciousness and *autonomía*, 71, 94–95, 112–13, 118

Peña, Devon, 19, 159n11; *autonomía*, 104; women's mobilizing and organizing, 144

Peña, Milagros: concept of "fe-enmi-misma," 94

Pleyers, Geoffrey, 98
poblado, 100, 103
Política Popular, 63
Porfiriato, 31, 47
Portillo, President José López, 36
PROCAMPO, 43
Programa Nacional Fronterizo (PRONAF), 54–55
Programa Nacional de Solidaridad (PRONASOL), 38–39
PROGRESA/Oportunidades, 43–44
Proletarian Line, 63–64

Quijano, Aníbal, 32–33

railroads, 53
reproductive labor, 17, 40, 44, 161n9
Rosa Emilia, 50, 74
Ruffo, Appel, Ernesto, 50; No Invasiones campaign, 51

Salinas de Gortari, President Carlos, 38–40, 47, 117; election of, 160n5
Samsung, 68, 79
San Diego/Tijuana border, 6, 18, 25, 45, 47; *encuentro*, 139; historical context, 54
Sandoval, Chela, 79
Sassen, Saskia, 23, 41; on citizenship, 123–24
Schmidt Camacho, Alicia, 101
Schnorr, Michael, 135, 138; photograph of, 135

school construction, 76
Segato, Rita Laura, 46
Shiva, Vandana, 14
Sitrin, Marina, 67
Smith, Andrea: political organizing,
    142; role of citizenship, 101
Sonoran Corridor: women's vulner-
    abilities, 45
Speed, Shannon, Aída Hernandez
    Castillo, and Lynn Stephen, 86
Stahler-Sholk, Richard, 102, 142
Starr, Amory, and Jason Adams:
    autonomy, 98–99
the State, 20, 23, 157n12; denial of
    rights, 76–77; displacement and
    removal by, 51; influence on
    women workers and children,
    111–13; regularized life by, 126,
    162n1
State Commission of Public Services
    of Tijuana (Comisión Estatal de
    Servicios Públicos de Tijuana,
    CESPT), 14, 81
Stavenhagen, Rodolfo, 31, 102
Stephen, Lynn, 16, 64
Stone-Mediatore, Shari, 9
structural violence, 13–17, 20, 39, 84,
    115, 140; and *autonomía*, 30; gender
    and, 24, 29, 35, 41, 57, 96, 105
Subcomandante Marcos, 4, 103
Sylvia, 9, 60–1; reflections on arrival
    to Maclovio Rojas, 127; on *necesi-
    dad*, 110

Terán Terán, Hector, 72
Teresa, 9, 81–82; oppositional con-
    sciousness, 95, 113; on unity, 126
testimonio, 9, 157n13
Tohono O'odham, 8
transnational feminist networks,
    22, 113

Treaty of Guadalupe Hidalgo, 53

Unión Nacional de Organizaciones
    Regionales Campesinas Autóno-
    mas (National Union of Autono-
    mous Regional Peasant Organi-
    zations, or UNORCA), 64
Unión de Posesionarios (Union of
    Possessors), 28
urban popular movements (UPMs),
    24, 64–5, 80; central role of
    women, 66, 111
U.S.-Mexico border, 20, 22; free
    trade, 45, 55; genealogy of
    neglect, 131; map of, 28; trans-
    border activism, 75, 134, 156n3;
    Sayak Valencia and "gore capi-
    talism," 122, 158n8, 164n1
U.S./Mexico/Central American
    Agreement (USMCA), 131

La Vía Campesina, 99
la vivienda, 9

Wallerstein, Immanuel, 32

Yorba family, 47

Zapatista Army of National Liber-
    ation (EZLN): comparison with
    Hortensia Hernández, 103, 121;
    Frente Zapatista de Libera-
    cion Nacional (FZLN), 156n8;
    National Democratic Conven-
    tion, 156n9
Zapatista movement: alter-
    globalization, 11, 15, 98; caravan,
    5; La Consulta, 155n3; National
    Democratic Convention, 156n9;
    parallels with Maclovio Rojas,
    102–103, 120–21; relationship to

the State, 104, 122; uprising of
January 1, 1994, 42, 158n2
Zapatour, 4

Zedillo, President Ernesto, 42–43
Zócalo, Mexico City, 5

About the Author

Michelle Téllez, an associate professor in the Department of Mexican American Studies at the University of Arizona, writes about transnational community formations, Chicana feminism, and gendered migration. A founding member of the Chicana M(other)work Collective, the Arizona Son Jarocho Collective, and the Binational Arts Residency project, Téllez has a long history in grassroots organizing projects and community-based arts and performance. She co-edited *The Chicana M(other)work Anthology: Porque Sin Madres No Hay Revolución*.